GRASS ROOTS

POLITICS NATIONAL

VOTING BEHAVIOR OF TYPICAL

STATES   BY HAROLD F. GOSNELL

NEW YORK / RUSSELL & RUSSELL

COPYRIGHT, 1942, BY AMERICAN COUNCIL ON PUBLIC AFFAIRS

REISSUED, 1970, BY RUSSELL & RUSSELL

A DIVISION OF ATHENEUM PUBLISHERS, INC.

BY ARRANGEMENT WITH PUBLIC AFFAIRS PRESS

L. C. CATALOG CARD NO: 71-102495

PRINTED IN THE UNITED STATES OF AMERICA

PREFACE

THIS study of American politics was started some years ago and has been carried on since that time with funds made available by the Social Science Research Committee of the University of Chicago. From an ideal standpoint it would be desirable to analyze many more than the six states covered herein and to investigate each state more intensively, but the main outlines of the pattern of national politics may be traced from the sample presented. In the states studied, those counties which resembled each other as to economic and social composition tended to behave in the same fashion politically. Thus, the dairy sections of Wisconsin and Northern Illinois were anti-New Deal, the corn belts of Iowa and Illinois were loosened from their Republican moorings of the 1920's, the coal mining sections of Pennsylvania and Illinois were strongly New Deal and remained so during the 1930's, and the larger cities of the North showed a marked leaning toward the Democratic party.

In making this study the author wishes to express his gratitude for the invaluable aid rendered by Dr. Samuel A. Stouffer, Dr. Natan C. Leites, Miss Margaret J. Schmidt, and the following graduate students: William G. Colman, who assisted in the preparation of Chapter III; Morris H. Cohen, who assisted in the preparation of Chapters IV and VI, and in the collection of materials for Chapter VII; Norman M. Pearson, who assisted in the preparation of Chapter V, and with Harold Elsten helped in the preliminary stages of Chapter IV; Alfred DeGrazia, who assisted in the preparation of Chapter VIII; and Sebastian DeGrazia, who assisted in the preparation of Chapter I.

A number of indispensable persons on the very efficient staff of the Social Science Research Committee have also done splendid work in connection with the production of the manuscript. Particular mention should be made of Miss Diane Greeter and Miss Alice Starr. Many NYA students, it should be noted, have performed functions which it is hoped have been as educational to them as they were helpful to the author. For the final text the author assumes full responsibility.

The author is indebted to the University of Chicago Press for permission to quote freely from his ''The Future of the American Party System'' which appeared as Chapter VI in *The Future of Government in the United States: Essays in Honor of Charles E. Merriam.* The editors of the *American Political Science Review,* the *Public Opinion Quarterly,* and the *Journal of Social Psychology* also kindly consented to the use of materials apearing in their respective journals.

HAROLD F. GOSNELL

CONTENTS

GRASS ROOTS POLITICS

CHAPTER I

STRAW BALLOTS VERSUS REAL BALLOTS

HOW may American politics be examined at its grass roots? The poll takers say, "Go out and talk with the voters and report your findings as we do." At first sight it might seem that the use of public opinion polls to find out what political parties are like is not only a simpler but a more direct method than the analysis of election returns. Interviewers ask selected persons how they are going to vote and then note their characteristics. If the sample of prospective voters is well chosen and carefully interviewed, then it may be used to describe the whole electorate. Of course it may be argued that non-voting, election manipulation, vote frauds, election-day pressure, and other well-known features of American politics may render the voting process a no better index of public opinion than the poll itself. On the other hand, the best of the final polls and the final election returns are now so close to

1

each other that it is justifiable to say that they are both measuring practically the same pattern of behavior.

Polls are useful in describing the party system because in a number of senses they are ballots with the social characteristics of the voters attached. The poll takers, besides seeking to ascertain the respondents' preferences on issues or men, make inquiries or judgments concerning their economic, religious, and occupational status; union membership, race, age, and sex; and educational, territorial, and political groupings. Insofar as the polls approximate the social situation of balloting, their data are useful in trying to find out what kind of voters support each of the major parties.

In some important particulars, however, a poll differs from an actual election. In the United States, the act of voting has been made more or less impersonal in order to safeguard the secrecy of the ballot. In general, the voter marks a ballot or pulls a lever on a machine in privacy, but a poll involves a face-to-face relationship. Every interpersonal relationship involves complex social pressures which may distort the results of an interview.[1]

The most ambitious of the polls in 1940 was that of the American Institute on Public Opinion—*i.e.*, George Gallup's poll—which attempted to predict the Democratic percentage in each state. While Gallup's average state error was very small, he consistently underestimated Roosevelt's popularity, except in the South, and as a result, his returns misplaced the electoral vote of eight important states. However, the election was so close that prediction was a hazardous task.

The Gallup surveys are useful for throwing light upon the behavior of the American voters, since they give the Roosevelt percentages of the two-party vote in 1936 and 1940 by various subgroupings.[2] Broken down by income and occupational groups, they indicate strong class differences between the two major parties and the tendency of these differences to increase during Roosevelt's second term. Neither in 1936 nor in 1940 did Roosevelt carry the upper income group, the businessmen, or the professional group, but in 1940 he ran farther behind among these groups than in 1936. In the upper income group, his popularity dropped from 42 per cent of the major party vote polled in 1936 to 28 per cent in 1940, a decline of 14 points. On the other hand, Roosevelt's popularity in the lower income group remained at a comparatively high level in both elections, declining only 7 points in 1940. In the lower income group, 76 per cent of the major party vote went to Roosevelt in 1936 and 69 per cent in 1940. Since the biases of the polls tended to underestimate the popularity of the New Deal, the spread between the lowest and the highest income groups is probably greater than is indicated by the poll returns. During his second term, Roosevelt's popularity declined most among the businessmen and white collar workers and least among the farmers. However, a special tabulation of the Midwest farmers indicated that their defection in 1940 was as great as that of the businessmen. Nationally, Roosevelt carried the farm vote in both elections but he lost the Midwest farmers in 1940. Among the relief recipients, his vote showed the least change. According to the poll figures, he received 84 per cent of the relief vote in 1936 and 80 per cent in 1940. It is probable that the Democratic leanings of the relief recipients were underestimated. During the 1940 campaign unfavorable publicity was given to the proposition that all reliefers and W.P.A. workers were to be reckoned as ''sure Roosevelt votes.'' Respondents in these groups resented being asked their preferences and tended to conceal or disort their views on the candidates.

Roosevelt's popularity among the trade union members was high in both elections, according to Gallup's figures. Eighty per cent of all union members interviewed in 1936 said that they were going to support Roosevelt. Four years later 72 per cent of the group indicated the same preference. The decline was exactly the same as the average for the entire country. In spite of John L. Lewis' stand for Willkie, the C.I.O. union members shifted less than any of the other labor groups.

The presidential preferences of Gallup's respondents in 1936 and 1940 were also broken down by religious groups. In both elections Roosevelt was most popular with Catholics, Jews, and nonchurch

members. He barely carried the Protestant vote in 1936 and lost it
in 1940. While the Catholic vote was heavy in 1936 (81 per cent),
the 13 per cent decline in 1940 was the largest of all the religious
groups. Among the Jewish people, Roosevelt maintained his popularity better than among any other religious group and this situation
may in part be traced to the Democrats' vigorous denunciation of
anti-Semitism. In the 1940 poll, 87 per cent of the Jewish respondents said that they were going to vote for Roosevelt. On the other
hand, the decline of the Democratic vote among the Catholics may
be attributed in part to the inclinations of the German-American
and Italian-American voters to favor Willkie because they thought
that his party was isolationist.

Gallup's poll of the Negroes was the most unsatisfactory of all of
his group polls. His survey shows that there was a decline in Roosevelt's popularity among Negro voters in 1940 as compared with 1936.
An analysis of the actual election returns for certain areas of Negro
concentration in northern cities for the two elections does not bear
out the trend shown by the poll figures.[3] In Chicago and Detroit
there was an actual increase in Roosevelt's vote in 1940. This shift
toward the Democratic party may be attributed to the importance
of the relief situation among Negro voters, the breaking up of stereo-
typed and traditional allegiances under the influences of urbanization, the changing attitude of the Democratic party toward Negroes,
growing class-consciousness, and the increasing pressure exercised
by the local party machines. Gallup's methods did not catch this
shift. Until 1933 it was generally expected that the Negroes would
vote Republican. Even after that, traditional Republicanism remained strong among the older Negroes. Experience in other surveys indicates that the Negroes interviewed showed a strong reluc-
tance to give information about their politics and would often
conceal or distort their views.

Estimates of the traditional vote from public opinion poll figures
present other difficulties. Since the lower income groups, the Negroes, and the foreign born groups tend to conceal their views, the
traditional Democratic vote may be underestimated. In 1940 Gallup

estimated that two-thirds of the voters were traditional voters, *i.e.*, they supported the same party in 1940 that they did in 1936; one-tenth were first voters (too young to vote in 1936); one-tenth failed to vote in 1936; and the remainder were largely persons who shifted from the Democratic to the Republican party. According to these figures, the 1940 election would have been very close if only those who were voters in 1936 had been counted, but Roosevelt won a large majority of the new voters and of those who failed to vote in 1936.

As compared with actual elections, the polls suffer because of the skepticism of the general public. Because they consider the polls unimportant, many persons do not seriously consider the questions submitted to them. They frequently take the view that "straw polls do not count" and sometimes answer the questions carelessly or erroneously. In some cases the interviewer may actually meet with antagonism. He may be rebuffed as a stranger, an outsider, one who should keep out of other people's affairs. This attitude is illustrated in the following statements appearing in a Louisiana newspaper:

Three months ago a half dozen post-graduate ''Social Science Workers'' from Princeton University, augmented by seven or eight East Side New Yorkers who had never in their lives seen a possum, tasted a sweet potato or chewed a plug of tobacco, arrived in New Orleans to conduct a so-called ''survey of public opinion.''

A friend up in Bienville Parish wrote that he was visited by a smart aleck Harlem nigger wearing a double-breasted suit and talking with a Harvard ''a'' who wanted to find out how people were going to vote.[4]

CHAPTER II

THE NATION AND THE STATES

THE PUBLIC opinion polls give some indication of the composition of parties and the nature of political trends in the United States, but they are no substitute for the election returns. In every election since the initiation of polls, the final election figures have held many surprises for the poll takers. We are justified, therefore, in falling back upon the official reports in investigating the character of American politics.

An examination of national election returns for the United States since 1896 shows that in American politics, as in British politics and in the politics of other democratic countries, the so-called law of the pendulum is manifested.[1] One way of defining this law, or generalization, is to say that after one set of government officials has been in office for a certain length of time a reaction develops against that set

6

and the popularity of its rivals increases to a point where the officials are displaced. The cycle is complete when the displaced party comes back into power. The party out of power promises favors which it is not likely to be able to grant, while the party in power must take the blame for conditions which it may, or may not, have helped to create. Without the possibility of a minority party becoming a majority party the democratic system could not exist, for an essential part of the system is the positive belief in the desirability of replacing one government with another by peaceful methods. It is to be expected, then, that the popularity of the major political parties will oscillate. The period and amplitude of the state oscillations, as compared with national trends, will be discussed in the pages which follow.

It is first necessary to consider the swing of the pendulum in American presidential elections from 1896 to 1940. Figure 1, which shows the rise and fall of the Democratic party expressed as a percentage of the combined Democratic and Republican vote, gives a general idea of the situation.[2] The inverse of this chart reveals the fortunes of the Republican party in that the low points of the graph represent the peaks of Republican popularity.

During the forty-five years following the crucial election of 1896 the Republican party enjoyed a longer period of success than did the Democratic. For twenty-eight years the Republicans held power, while the Democrats were in control for twenty; the ratio of electoral success was seven to five. However, it is interesting to note that the relative magnitude of the Democratic successes in the thirties was equal to that of the Republican successes at the turn of the century and in the twenties, in spite of the fact that after the disastrous defeats of 1920 and 1924 many dire prophesies were made about the decline of the Democratic party.[3] The 1920 decade was a boom period and it was difficult, under the circumstances, for the party out of power to convince the voters that they were suffering hardships because of a Republican administration in Washington. The depression of the thirties dispelled the myth of "Republican prosperity" and gave the Democrats chance to establish themselves, for a period, as the party of the underprivileged. Whether the 1940 election, which

DEMOCRATIC PERCENTAGE OF TWO-PARTY AND TOTAL PRESIDENTIAL VOTES, 1896-1940

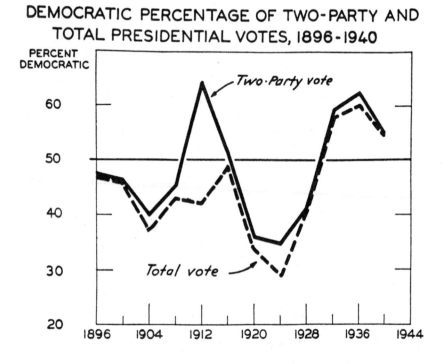

Figure 1

marked a slight decline in Roosevelt's popularity, indicates the beginning of a new cycle likely to return the Republican party in 1944
is still problematical. The congressional elections of 1942 and the public opinion polls will be helpful in resolving this question. If we go
back farther in American party history, it will be seen that the amplitude of national swings have varied from sixteen to twenty-four
years. The duration of the present political cycle is unknown, but
the chances are that it will not exceed a quarter of a century.[4]

To explain the ups and downs of the two major parties in the
United States since 1896 would require more space than can be provided here. The subject, though not adequately treated, has been
touched upon by various writers.[5] The present study does not pur-
port to be a party history. It is rather an analysis of the composition of American parties—the sorting process of party politics[6] in
which only the broadest trends can be considered.

The relationship between economic and political cycles is, of course,
significant.[7] It may be said that during a period of economic contraction there is likely to be a change in the party controlling the White
House. During the period from 1896 to the present this rule has
held true for every presidential election except those of 1900 and 1912.
International complications aided the Republican party in 1900, when
McKinley was returned to the presidency, in spite of the fact that
there had been fifteen months of contraction prior to the election. In
1912 the Republican party lost—although the business curve was
rising—because it was torn by internal strife involving policies and
personalities. Furthermore, the depression of 1900 has been called a
business man's panic; the bankers and speculators were much more
affected than the public in general. In ten out of the last twelve presidential elections, economic conditions appear to be predominant factors, prosperity deterring and depression aiding a change in the party
controlling the presidency.

The elections of 1900, 1916, 1920 and 1940 indicate that an international crisis may have considerable influence upon the fortunes of
the major parties.[8] In 1900 the issue of imperialism overshadowed
other questions and the Republican candidate probably benefited by

the general feeling that the country was in the middle of a stream and it was not advisable to swap horses. Even Bryan, who was opposed to imperialism, refused to make the most of the issue because the country was committed to a given policy. Sixteen years later the World War overshadowed American politics and Wilson was reelected—in part because many people believed the widely disseminated Democratic slogan, "He kept us out of war." Four years later the foreign relations of the United States reacted strongly against the Democratic party. The debates on the Versailles treaty and the League of Nations greatly strengthened isolationist sentiment, and this was capitalized by the Republican party. In 1940 American foreign policy was again a major issue, this time the stand of the Democratic administration being the one most widely held. The public opinion polls indicate clearly that a majority of the American people wished to give all possible aid to Great Britain. It might be argued that in the absence of the international crisis the Republican party might have won the presidency. On three of the four occasions listed above, the international tension tended to accentuate political changes which were closely associated with economic conditions. Only in 1900 were business trends moving in a direction opposed to the fortunes of the party which was aided by the crisis in foreign relations. It is therefore difficult to evaluate the relative pulling power of these two influences—internal economic conditions and international relations—upon the voters.

A third influence which has a powerful effect upon the major party vote is domestic political crisis. Factional warfare within one of the major parties may have a disastrous effect upon its electoral position. This was the situation in 1912, when the conservative leaders of the Republican party preferred defeat at the polls to the return of Theodore Roosevelt to power. The split in the Republican ranks made the election of Woodrow Wilson inevitable. The breach was not entirely healed by 1916 and in that year also Wilson and the Democrats were the beneficiaries.

National returns only indicate the broadest trends in voting behavior. The election results, state by state, are needed in attempting to isolate the various influences which are at work in the electoral process. By setting up significant hypotheses, it is possible to get striking corroboration by merely comparing the voting trends in each state with the national trends. In this connection special attention should be called to *Ballot Behavior*, a study by Louis Bean issued by the American Council on Public Affairs in 1940. Charts similar to Figure 1 have been made for each of the forty-eight states by Mr. Bean.[9] They show the striking similarity between the political oscillations of the states and the nation as a whole, except in the Solid South, where there is an entirely different pattern. But the northern and western states show important variations as well as a general similarity. In seeking satisfactory explanations for these variations it is possible to test a number of theories about political behavior in the United States.[10]

If each state chart were drawn on transparent paper and then superimposed upon a national chart of the same scale, it would be discovered that the chart for Ohio comes the closest to the national one. This might be interpreted in a variety of ways. It might mean that the Ohio voters present a typical cross section of the national electorate and that they respond to campaign stimuli in about the same fashion as all the voters outside of the state. If this were the case there would, by inference, be no peculiar influences at work in Ohio.

A similar comparison for each of the states would show that for the period 1895-1940 they could be roughly grouped in four classes:[11]

1. States (such as Ohio) which parallel national trends, although some tend to favor one major party and others its rival.
2. States that swing with the nation but more violently; some of these tend to favor one major party and others its opponent.
3. States which swing with the nation but less violently (these might be called the conservative or stabilized states).
4. States (such as those in the Solid South) that show no relation to national trends but constitute a group by themselves.

Each of these four groups will be discussed in greater detail in the pages which follow. The geographical distribution of the groups is shown in Figure 2.

VOTING TRENDS IN PRESIDENTIAL ELECTIONS, 1896-1936

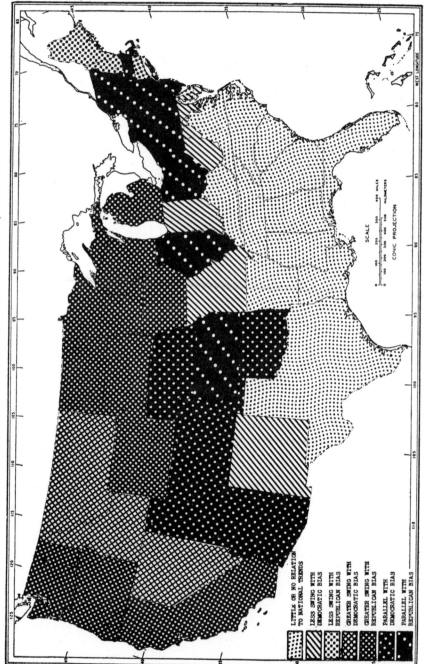

Figure 2

States Which Parallel National Trends

The typical states, those which move in the same direction as the nation as a whole, are discussed first. According to the method described above and various other indices, Ohio is the most typical of all.[12] On the average, it is most likely to go as the nation goes. The state was relatively lukewarm toward John W. Davis in 1924, toward Al Smith in 1928, and toward Franklin D. Roosevelt in 1932, but on the other hand it was relatively enthusiastic in 1920 about its Democratic native son candidate, Governor James M. Cox, and about President Wilson's re-election in 1916. In the other elections the Democratic percentage for Ohio was almost identical with but slightly under the national Democratic percentage.[13]

Twelve other states might be placed in the same general category of typical states, although none come as close as Ohio to the national trend. Like Ohio, seven of these—Massachusetts, Vermont, New Jersey, New York, Pennsylvania, Kansas, and Illinois—have a Republican bias, and five—Oklahoma, Colorado, Utah, Arizona, and Nebraska—have a Democratic bias.[14] Except for 1924 when the Democratic candidate, Davis, was a native son, West Virginia also fits into this category.[15]

Because of its importance, something might well be said about the relationship of the state of New York to national trends. Except for the elections of 1904 and 1928, when native son Democratic candidates were running, New York has always been slightly more Republican than the nation as a whole. If allowance is made for this bias, New York may be said to belong to the "parallel" group.

This analysis brings out clearly the pulling power of a native son candidacy. A state which has a native son candidate invariably gives him a larger vote than would be "normally" expected, unless, of course, both major party candidates are natives of the same state. This situation occurred during the period under review only in 1904 and 1920.[16]

States With Greater Swing

There are thirteen states whose voting charts resemble the national one, but the swings are more pronounced than in the country as a whole.[17] When the nation was Republican, these states were among those most strongly Republican, and when the nation swung to the Democratic party they became the most strongly Democratic. It is significant that all of them are in the West and North Central portions of the United States. These states can be counted upon to fluctuate violently. In this region party labels have less meaning than elsewhere in the United States, and third party movements, insurgent movements in party primaries, and progressive party leaders with long periods of public service are characteristic.

Ten of these states—Michigan, Wisconsin, Iowa, Minnesota, South Dakota, North Dakota, Wyoming, Washington, Oregon, and California[18]—had a Republican bias during the period under discussion. For the nation as a whole the average Democratic percentage of votes was 46.5 and for each of the ten states it was 5 per cent or more below this figure.

This group of states marks a rather definite political pattern. At the beginning of the period (1896), Bryan was more popular here than in the country at large, but his popularity declined rapidly in his second and third campaigns for the presidency. When the Democrats put up a conservative candidate, they suffered greatly in these states, particularly in 1904 and 1924. Any candidate who carried a banner of Progressivism did well in the corn belt, winter wheat, Mountain, and Pacific coastal area. This was true of Theodore Roosevelt as a Republican and a Progressive, of La Follette as a Progressive in 1924, and of various self-styled home state Progressives. While Woodrow Wilson was relatively popular in this region, it was Franklin D. Roosevelt and his New Deal program which brought the Democratic tide to its fullest flood.

Three states in this region—Montana, Idaho, and Nevada—showed a larger swing than the country at large, but their basic tendencies were Democratic, except during the twenties.[19] These Mountain states went strongly for Bryan every time he ran for the presidency, but they had little use in 1904 for Parker, an eastern sound money man, or for John W. Davis, an eastern corporation lawyer with Wall Street connections, in 1924; Idaho was also relatively cool toward Cox, a publisher who went contrary to the isolationism of its favorite son, Senator William E. Borah, and toward Al Smith who was thought to know less about farm problems than that product of the Iowa soil, Herbert Clark Hoover.

Five of the states listed in the above—Wyoming, Washington, Nevada, Montana, Idaho—and the so-called typical states Colorado and Utah were silver mining states, and it was these seven which showed a much higher Democratic vote in 1896 than they did in 1900. The "silver bloc" continued its peculiar brand of politics throughout the period under discussion.

States With Less Swing

There is a definite group of states which follow national trends but they are slower to move and do not swing as far as the country as a whole. Here the habits of traditional voting are deeply rooted. Other states may hasten to get on the bandwagon, but these take their time. The voters do not immediately accept some new program or some glamorous personality; they stick by their tried and true party mentors for a little while longer than do the voters in other states. As in the case of the states in the other groupings, some have Republican and some have Democratic basic tendencies.

Any one who is familiar with American national politics might anticipate that the relatively more stabilized Republican states would be found in the Northeast. Four New England states—Maine, New Hampshire, Connecticut, and Rhode Island—and Delaware fit into the category.[20] Bryan was very unpopular here each time he ran; relatively speaking, those legal representatives of big business, Parker and Davis, did not fare so badly here; and the personality of Roosevelt did not seem at all charming in 1932 and 1936 to many New Englanders who had known him as a Groton scholar, a Harvard man, a summer vacationer, and an amateur yatchsman. It was only in 1940 when Roosevelt appeared as the candidate more likely to pursue a vigorous policy on national defense that New England turned to him.[21] On the other hand, the popularity of Al Smith in this region was phenomenal. The voters of foreign extraction in New England were attracted by his Catholic faith, his immigrant background, his humble beginning, or his accent.

The net result of these various conflicting tendencies was that, when the fortunes of the Democratic party sunk to a low level in the country as a whole—1904, 1920, 1924, and 1928—they did not drop quite so low in the above five states as elsewhere. When they rose in the nation as a whole—in 1912, 1916, 1932, and 1936—they did not soar as high here as elsewhere. One qualification must be made to this statement. In Delaware Al Smith did not fare as well as might have been expected. Apparently the Du Ponts did not like his brand of urban progressivism. If Al had been the Democratic nominee in 1936 he would undoubtedly have done better in this region than he did in 1928.

Skipping across the country, we find another group of relatively stable states with basic Democratic tendencies—Maryland, West Virginia, Indiana, Missouri, and New Mexico. Although these states are not contiguous and they vary in the strength of Democratic bias, they are enough alike to be classed together.[22] In none did the Democratic vote fall below 40 per cent, which means that the Democratic lines held pretty well during the twenties, when the Democratic forces were shattered in other states. Parker's nomination in 1904 did not prove disruptive in these states, and the New Deal vote was average or even below normal, as in Indiana.

Persons well versed in American politics may wonder why Indiana is placed in this category. Should it not be classified among the "parallel" states? Is it not more Republican than Democratic? The lines between the parallel and stabilized states are not hard and fast.[23] However, there is no avoiding the fact that Indiana's deviations from the normal have been in the direction of stability. Both the Republican and Democratic party organizations in Indiana have been able to hold a relatively large number of their supporters in time of stress. The state has had such master organizers as Will Hays on the Republican side and Tom Taggart on the Democratic.

States With No Relation to National Trends

As indicated above, the group of states which has no relation to
the national political cycles is found in the South. A few might be
put into the preceding category of states which do not swing as far as
the country as a whole. This is especially true of North Carolina and
the border states, Kentucky and Tennessee.[24] However, the other
southern states have a unique pattern. In Virginia, for example,
Davis was about as popular as Roosevelt and Bryan's popularity increased in his successive campaigns. The low point in the Democratic
vote was reached in 1928, when the native white Protestants revolted
against that product of New York's East Side parochial schools, the
"dripping wet" Al Smith. With the exception of this election, im-
mobility is the chief characteristic of the South.

Religion as a Factor

It is now possible by recombining the states in another fashion to
get an approximate idea of the importance of religious considerations
in American politics. This question was raised most dramatically in
the presidential election of 1928 when Al Smith, a Catholic, was nominated by the Democratic party. Is there any relationship between
Smith's vote by states and the proportion of Catholics in the population? At first sight, it would seem difficult to establish a relationship,
but a closer examination shows that in 1928 those states which had a
high proportion of Catholics showed an unusually high vote for Smith
as compared with the "normal" Democratic vote, while those states
which had a high proportion of Protestants showed an abnormally low
Democratic vote. Thus, in Massachusetts, where two-thirds of the
church membership was Catholic, Smith's vote was 15 per cent higher
than what would be normally expected, and in Virginia, where only
3 per cent of the church membership was Catholic, Smith's vote was
20 per cent below what would have been "normal" had a Protestant
been a candidate.

General Observations

An examination of the election returns for the states and the nation as a whole shows that changes in American politics are usually not abrupt. There is a gradual shift from one phase of the political cycle to another. Thus, after World War I the tide of Democratic fortunes began to turn in 1928 when the Democratic candidate lost but polled a good vote. The national political tides ebb and flow with changes in business conditions and in the international situation, and shifts in the control of the party organizations. State political tides come and go with changes in political personalities, in issues which affect the economy of the states directly, and in social issues which have peculiar importance to the culture of the communities concerned.

The state and national results show the above general trends, but it is necessary to examine the returns by counties in a number of states to get a closer view of American politics.

PRESIDENTIAL ELECTION, 1936

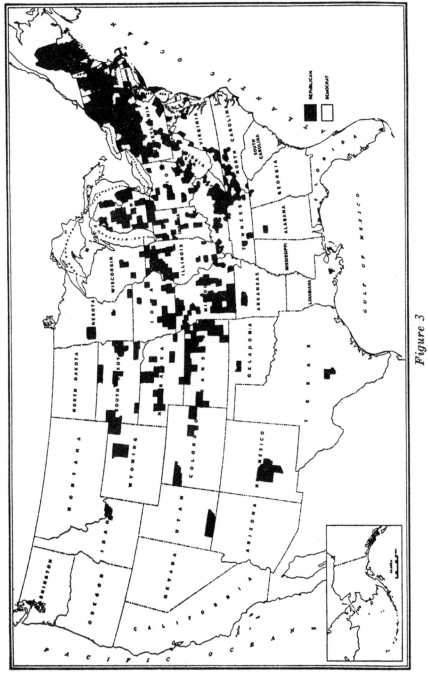

Figure 3

PRESIDENTIAL ELECTION, 1940

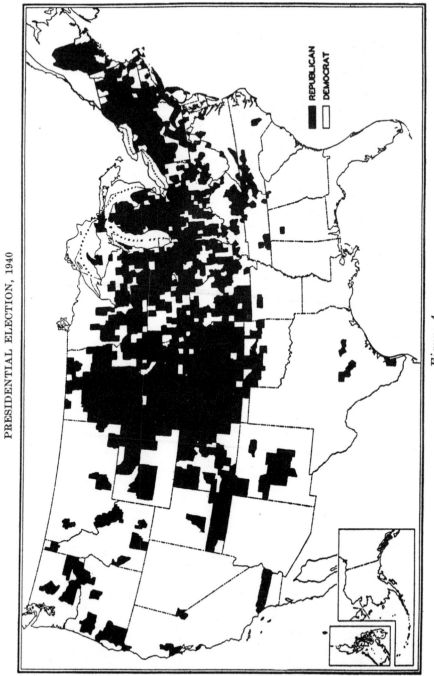

Figure 4

CHAPTER III

INDUSTRIAL POLITICS: PENNSYLVANIA

DURING the 1930's the treatment of economic issues in political campaigns moved from the general to the particular. Prior to 1928, the issues of the protective tariff, free coinage of silver, cancellation of war debts and "trust busting" were widely and heatedly debated, but the attitude of many voters toward these questions was largely determined by the family tradition of party affiliation. As long as economic conditions were good, many workers in industries which were not benefited by high tariffs supported protection in general. The definite results of a tariff or monetary policy were concealed from the ordinary voter, and in the absence of better information he tended to believe what the press and the politicians told him about the economic effects of this or that governmental policy.

Beginning with the stock market debacle of October, 1929, the relation between economic conditions and public policies became clearer to a larger number of voters. If the voter was a farmer, he saw his income declining more rapidly than that of the city dweller; perhaps his farm was sold on the courthouse steps to satisfy interest and taxes. If the voter was an urban laborer, he or his friends may have lost their jobs, gone on relief, or moved from one makeshift shanty "Hooverville" to another. Although these voters held no definite view about the specific policies which had produced these conditions, they were concretely aware of governmental inaction. In 1932 they voted against inaction and for change, discarding in the process their traditional party affiliations.

With the advent of the New Deal, many more voters became aware of the importance of governmental policies in the economic sphere. If the voter were a farmer producing crops within the scope of the AAA program, he received his checks for crop reduction. If he were an industrial worker, he perhaps received a wage increase (as a result of the New Deal labor legislation encouraging unionization), unemployment compensation if temporarily unemployed, or a WPA job if out of work for some time. If he were a businessman, he saw social security pay roll and other taxes cut into his margin of profit. Everywhere the voter was brought face to face with the effects of governmental economic policies upon his daily life.

Whether one is for or against the New Deal, he will certainly concede that the economic era of the twenties is gone forever and that government under future administrations will devote more attention to economic matters. In view of the increasing importance of economic issues in political campaigns, it is pertinent to study the recent relationship between political and economic trends in one of the leading industrial states—Pennsylvania. An analysis of the voting behavior of the industrial states during the period 1896-1940 shows that they fall into a distinct political pattern. As compared with the country as a whole they have been more Republican, but when allowance is made for this tendency it is clear that they have closely paralleled national trends.[1] The old saying, "As Maine goes, so goes the Nation," should be changed to read, "As the industrial Northeast shifts in politics, so shifts the Nation."

Pennsylvania is typical of the industrial states which have paralleled national trends during the period 1896-1940, but with a distinct Republican bias.[2] The relative strength of the two major parties in this state, as shown by the presidential vote, has fairly closely resembled the national picture when 6 to 8 per cent is added to the Democratic side to allow for Republican predilections.

In describing the politics of Pennsylvania, the great strength of the Republican party is usually emphasized. It is true that the state did not go Democratic in presidential elections during the long period from 1856 (when James Buchanan, a Democrat, and the only Pennsylvanian to occupy the White House, was elected) until 1936, but this does not mean that Pennsylvania did not move with the political tides that swept the nation. In 1882 and 1890, Democratic governors were elected; in 1912 Theodore Roosevelt carried the state as the Progressive candidate for President; and in 1928 Al Smith polled the largest vote ever received by any Democratic candidate in Pennsylvania up to that time.

The extent of the national political upheavel in the 1930's is clearly illustrated by developments in Pennsylvania. In absolute numbers the Republican vote during the period 1924 to 1936 has varied from a million and a half to two millions, but the Democratic vote rose from 409,000 for Davis in 1924 to 2,354,000 for Roosevelt in 1936, nearly a sixfold increase. Within a margin of some five or six hundred thousand the Republican party managed to hold its vote, but the Democratic party attracted to its ranks not only the dissatisfied Republicans but a huge army of new voters—the young voters and those who had formerly been non-voters through indifference.

Although Hoover carried the state by a plurality of approximately 150,0000 in 1932, this election clearly showed the handwriting on the wall. The Republican demise was complete in 1934 when George H. Earle and Joseph E. Guffey, Democrats, were elected governor and United States senator, respectively. In 1936 President

Roosevelt, with strong labor support, carried Pennsylvania by approximately 650,000—the first time since the Civil War that Pennsylvania had cast a Democratic vote in the electoral college. Following a bitter primary fight, the Democratic reign met some severe reverses in 1938 when Governor Earle was defeated in his contest for the United States senatorship and his running mate lost the fight for the governorship. In Pennsylvania, as in other states, the pendulum was swinging back after the extraordinary elections of 1934 and 1936. However, in 1940 Pennsylvania for the second time cast its electoral vote for Roosevelt.

Economic Conditions and Pennsylvania Politics

An analysis of the study of the relationship between economic and political trends in Pennsylvania is of value because of the state's industrial importance. In manufactures it ranks second in the United States, yielding preeminence only to New York. The value of its manufactured products totaled over four billion dollars in 1931, or almost 10 per cent of the aggregate produced in the nation in that year.[3]

The major industries in Pennsylvania grew out of the discovery of iron ore and coal deposits. The early development of these minerals furnished fuel and basic metal for the iron furnaces, and rapid evolution in iron and steel manufacture and coal production has brought the state to a very strategic position in the industrial world. Her mineral industries employed about 600,000 persons in 1929, giving support to one-third of the state's total population.[4] The principal mineral products are coal, cement, natural gas, clay products, petroleum, and stone. Anthracite fields cover about 484 square miles in the eastern end of the state, contributing largely to the economic life of some nine counties.[5] Bituminous coal is mined in some sixteen counties in the western part of the state.[6] Pennsylvania is the largest producer of cement in the United States, and in some years has produced over half the country's total output. Most of the cement plants are in the Lehigh district, but there is also a group near Pittsburgh. In addition to the basic heavy industries, there are diversified manufacturing plants of every description. Finished metal products are made in all parts of the state; Pittsburgh has one of the largest electrical equipment plants in the world; and textiles are turned out in great quantities in Philadelphia and other eastern counties.

Not only is Pennsylvania an outstanding industrial state, but it also supports an agriculture of no mean proportions. The total land area is approximately 28,700,000 acres, of which slightly over 53 per cent was classified as farm land in 1930.[7] The remaining land is largely in urban centers and forests. The highest percentage of land in farms occurs in the southeastern and eastern areas, with the lowest percentage in the northwest central part along the Appalachian mountains. Livestock and livestock products account for two-thirds of the cash income of the farmers. The most prosperous agricultural counties are in the eastern part of the state, but agricultural pursuits are of more importance than industrial in some twenty-one counties, and they are of some importance in nearly every county except Philadelphia.[8]

If industrial and political democracy were equivalent, it is clear that the workers and farmers would long ago have been more active in the government of Pennsylvania. However, it has been difficult to implement the principle of majority rule because of the disparity between economic and political power. Political parties cannot be run without funds and in Pennsylvania it was taken for granted, until recently, that the bulk of the campaign funds would come from the leaders of the steel, oil, railroad, aluminum and other large-scale industries. The operation of this system in the first part of the twentieth century was graphically described by Senator Boies Penrose, the arch representative of big business: "Why not, if you would be a true friend of these dear people, make your alliances with the employers of the people, the strong men who understood the art of mating dollars and breeding millions? To whom did the reformers go when they needed the money to finance their campaigns of blither? To the wage earners? Not by a damn sight. They went to the capitalists, to great merchants and manufacturers who, as it happened, themselves yearned to own legislatures and write laws."[9]

Since the death of Senator Penrose in 1921, no political leader has risen who could manipulate the alliance between business and politics as well as he did. The advent of the New Deal in the thirties forced the politicians to turn to those very same wage earners whom Penrose had despised. Truly this was a revolution in the politics of industrial America.

One approach to the problem of the relationship between politics and economic conditions is to study the variation in the prosperity of different regions over a given period of time. The shifts in the economic index of a county may be related to the shifts in its vote. To secure an adequate measure of economic conditions by counties is a problem of considerable difficulty in a state of such diverse economy as Pennsylvania. Several alternatives presented themselves: (1) An index might be based upon the volume of industrial production or the extent of unemployment, neglecting the counties which were nearly entirely agricultural. (2) The sixty-seven counties might be classified as agricultural or industrial and each group treated separately. (3) A composite index might be worked out which would roughly indicate the relative economic situation of the entire county. The third course was followed and the relative importance of agriculture and industry (manufacturing and mining) was determined for each county by ascertaining the number of persons gainfully employed in each group as set forth in a classification of occupations in the 1930 census.

Index numbers were derived from the amount of wages and salaries paid in manufacturing enterprises[10] and the value of principal crops, livestock, milk, eggs, wool and honey,[11] for the period 1927-1937, with 1927-1928 being equal to 100. These index numbers of industrial and agricultural conditions were then weighted in proportion to the relative importance of the two types of pursuits in the particular county, as reflected in the weights described above. While the numbers so derived could be further refined by the inclusion of several other factors, they afford a general picture of the change in economic conditions within each county during the period 1927-1937.[12]

Since the index number indicates the change in economic conditions from the base years 1927-1928, it is necessary to relate voting behavior to it in terms of net shift in percentages from one election to another. Thus a comparison may be obtained of the change in economic conditions from 1928 to 1932 and the shift in Democratic vote for that period by relating the shift in index number to the net shift in vote.

The economic havoc wrought by the depression is reflected by comparing the index numbers of 1928 and 1932. Allegheny County dropped from 97.5 in 1928 to 41.7 in 1932, and Philadelphia from 100.3 to 57.8.[13] Pay rolls for the period June, 1929 to June, 1931 reflected a percentage decrease of 43.2 in manufacturing industries in the state.[14] Average weekly earnings of workers in manufacturing fell from a peak of $27.53 a week in May, 1929 to $21.25 in June, 1931, a 22.8 per cent decline.[15] The estimated number of unemployed in Pennsylvania for June, 1931 was approximately 919,000, or nearly 25 per cent of the total working population.[16] No doubt this number had increased considerably by November, 1932. The agricultural areas were likewise affected. The value of the agricultural products of Lancaster County declined from $39,404,550 in 1928 to $17,261,270 in 1932 and in Fulton County from $2,675,160 to $1,344,710.[17]

It might be expected that the mining areas would exhibit the greatest shift in vote from 1928 to 1932, due to the critical economic conditions prevailing in those districts in 1932. However, it must be remembered that these highly industrialized counties were the centers of Smith support in 1928, while the rural areas gave him the least support. Therefore, a greater shift would be more feasible in rural counties than in the densely populated mining areas. Of the ten counties displaying the greatest shift from 1928 to 1932, eight are definitely rural in composition. A definite relationship between the shift in vote and economic conditions is indicated by a comparison of the shift in index numbers and the shift in Democratic vote.[18] In other words, the greater the negative index shift, the greater the positive vote shift.

That the relationship is not close may be explained by the fact that the rural-farm, native-white areas had voted against Smith while the urban and foreign-born elements supported him. Since the effects of the depression were felt in all parts of the state, it may be shown that, in general, excluding the influence of the social factors which were strongly related to the Smith vote, the areas hardest hit shifted the most to Roosevelt. This further substantiates our earlier concept of the 1932 Roosevelt support as a protest vote against Hoover, the scapegoat in the bursting of the "New Era" bubble.[19]

In 1932 the voters of this traditionally Republican state flocked to the standard of Roosevelt, though not in sufficient numbers to prevent Hoover from carrying the state with the aid of a 70,000 majority in Philadelphia. With the advent of the national New Deal, the voters were soon given ample opportunity to evaluate Roosevelt's policies concretely. The NRA, AAA, CWA, and PWA followed in rapid succession. Pennsylvania's industrial pump, it was claimed, was sufficiently primed by these devices to effect the re-employment of thousands.

Immediately after his election in 1934, Governor Earle began to create a New Deal in Harrisburg to duplicate that at Washington.[20] The coal and steel police were abolished and several progressive labor measures were enacted. In 1936 the commonwealth exhibited its gratitude for economic betterment under the New Deal by presenting Roosevelt with a majority of over 600,000. Just what relationship existed between the upward trend of the business cycle and the shift toward Roosevelt? A comparison between the shift in index number and that in vote indicates the existence of a tendency for the counties which had enjoyed the greatest degree of economic improvement to shift markedly toward Roosevelt; the mean shift in Democratic vote, 1932-1936, is 6.23 compared to a shift in index number of 33.72—a positive shift in both cases. If allowance is made for the fact that the greatest shifts in the vote took place in the more urbanized counties, the relationship between the vote shift and the economic index is closer.[21] However, this does not mean that the industrial and mining counties having large relief and WPA rolls did not support Roosevelt in 1936. Of the twelve counties giving Roosevelt the largest vote in that year, all but one (Greene, traditionally Democratic) was definitely indus-trial.[22] But these counties were heavily for Roosevelt in 1932 and con-sequently did not shift as greatly toward him as did some of the semi-industrial and non-mining counties such as Delaware, which were luke-warm for him in 1932. The positive relationship found here is similar to that discovered in Iowa with reference to the shift in Roosevelt vote from 1932 to 1936.[23]

The analysis of the political behavior of industrial Pennsylvania by counties leaves much to be desired. Figures 5 and 6 show the coun-ty results for the 1932 and 1940 elections. Since a county is an arti-ficial unit which does not always coincide with economic and cultural areas, the county analysis has been supplemented by one based upon the economic regions as devised by the Pennsylvania State Planning Board. An analysis of the shifts in the Democratic strength from 1932 to 1936 in terms of these regions revealed the following:

1. The industrial regions were most intensely pro-Roosevelt in their shifts during this period.
2. The agricultural regions, such as the dairy, sheep raising, fruit and diversified farming ones, were those in which Roosevelt lost or else made only very moderate gains.
3. Two resort areas were characterized by a shift against Roose-velt.
4. Of the industrial and mining areas, the general anthracite coal region was only very moderate in its shift toward Roosevelt.
5. The sparsely settled forest region in the northwestern part of the state was rather pro-Roosevelt in its shift.

An interpretation of the figures shows that in general the shift toward Roosevelt was greatest where his support in 1932 had been the weakest. However, the dairy areas were an exception. His support here was low in 1932 and he actually lost votes in 1936. On the other hand, in the Pittsburgh industrial region, where his strength was al-ready great, he received considerable increases. President Roosevelt's vote in 1940 was on the average 5 per cent less in each of the Penn-sylvania counties than it was in 1936. The largest losses were in the sparsely settled forest region in the northwestern part of the state

PENNSYLVANIA—PERCENTAGE OF ROOSEVELT VOTE
TO TOTAL VOTE (BY COUNTIES) IN 1932

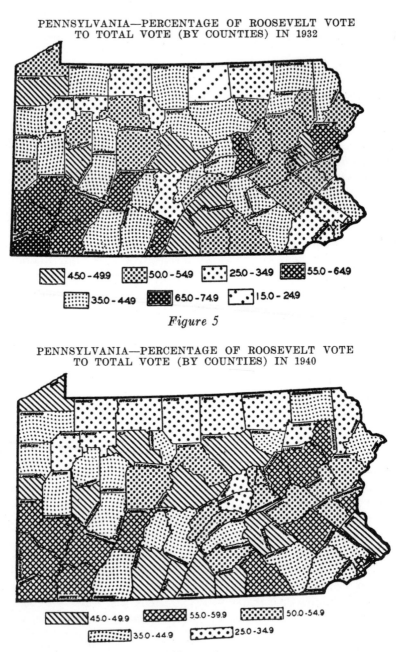

Figure 5

PENNSYLVANIA—PERCENTAGE OF ROOSEVELT VOTE
TO TOTAL VOTE (BY COUNTIES) IN 1940

Figure 6

and in the metropolitan region of Pittsburgh. The President held his own best in the hard coal region and in the dairy, sheep raising, fruit and diversified farming sections.

An analysis of the vote in 1936 was next made by degree of urbanization.[24] This clearly showed that Roosevelt's greatest strength in the 1936 election was in the two large metropolitan areas of Philadelphia and Pittsburgh. He was weakest in towns below 2,500 population and on the farms. The tabular analysis further substantiates the concept of the New Deal voting strength as being primarily urban and industrial.

The election of 1936 marked the peak of success for the Earle-Guffey-CIO-WPA machine. The United Mine Workers and the CIO had delivered in magnificent style,[25] with Roosevelt sweeping forty of the sixty-seven counties. The industrial upswing in early 1937 further enhanced the prestige of the party in power. Beginning with the recession in the summer of that year, a succession of events brought disaster to the state administration. Attorney General Charles J. Margiotti brought a series of graft charges against Governor Earle and State Democratic Chairman David Lawrence with the result that Margiotti was ousted by the governor.[26] The Democratic-labor alliance was split wide open in 1938 by the endorsement of Charles A. Jones for Governor by the State Democratic Committee in preference to Thomas Kennedy, Lieutenant Governor and Secretary-Treasurer of the United Mine Workers.[27] The primary election in May was exceedingly bitter with Margiotti entering the race as an independent candidate. Mud slinging was the order of the day. The disintegrating effect of the primary, in addition to the indictment of several Democratic leaders for bribery and grafting on state contracts, was undoubtedly instrumental in the defeat of the Democratic candidates in November, 1938. The fact that Jones, the Democratic candidate for governor, received a higher vote in practically all counties than did Earle for the senatorship is indicative of the fact that the charges against Earle had produced a negative public reaction.[28]

It is interesting to note that the counties which shifted most from the Democratic party in 1938 were non-mining industrial centers such as Dauphin and Delaware. On the other hand, the mining counties with large relief and WPA rolls tended to remain Democratic. Fayette, Lackawanna and Washington, all mining counties, were the only ones in which Earle received more than 50 per cent of the vote.

Because of the importance of the mining industry in Pennsylvania, the political activity of the CIO, and the concentration of the mining areas in certain counties, it was thought desirable to make a special analysis of the mining counties.[29] The analysis shows that they have been centers of Democratic strength in recent years. All have at least 25 per cent of their working population engaged in mining and have consistently come out more strongly for New Deal candidates than has the state as a whole. In 1940 the anthracite counties shifted less from the New Deal than did the bituminous counties. The tendency of the less prosperous areas to remain Democratic in 1938 is further borne out by an examination of the relationship between the per cent population on WPA rolls and the Earle vote for senator.[30] While the relationship is not close, it is present.

In summarizing economic motivations in voting behavior for the 1932, 1936, 1938 and 1940 elections, the following conclusions seem reasonably evident: (1) In the 1932 election, those counties which had been most adversely afflicted by the depression were strongest in their support of Roosevelt. (2) Counties which had enjoyed the most marked economic improvement tended to shift most heavily to Roosevelt in 1936, although his strongest support came from the mining areas which had large relief rolls. A distinction must be drawn between absolute support and positive shift; although the latter counties supported Roosevelt heavily in 1936, they showed less shift toward him than did areas which had been only lukewarm for him in 1932 (3) In 1938 economic motivation was rather obscure with the exception of the relief factor; the fact that a state and not a national election was involved and the beclouding of economic issues by factional quarrels in the Democratic party tends to produce this result. However, the analysis indicates a tendency for the WPA relief population to support the Democratic candidates. (4) Roosevelt's third candidacy brought an increase in the Democratic vote as compared with 1938 but the level fell below 1936. The figures indicate that the 1940 campaign attracted to the polls many voters who stayed at home in 1938. It is the author's opinion that the increase in the poll came from the lower economic groups. (5) Broadly speaking, the economic basis of New Deal support is more easily defined in general terms of the urban-labor-mining vote than in terms of economic deprivations and indulgences. However, the foregoing presentation seems to indicate general tendencies with respect to the latter terms. Areas which improved economically tended to express their gratitude to the New Deal; areas which were unaffected economically or became worse, but not to the point of widespread dependence on relief, were lukewarm to Roosevelt; but the blighted mining districts chose the Democratic party as the most likely straw to clutch at in their struggle for self-preservation.

The Influence of Social Conditions on Voting Behavior

Much has been said and written regarding the so-called capture by the New Deal of the urban and foreign-born vote in the North. The election of 1936 was termed by many a battle between rural areas and small towns on the one hand, and the political machines of the large cities on the other.[31]

Pennsylvania is typical of present-day industrial America; it ranks second to New York in population,[32] and only 8.8 per cent of the state's population live on farms.[33] Therefore, it is of particular interest to examine recent elections in Pennsylvania in the light of the above hypotheses. It might be assumed that conclusions resulting from the following analysis would likewise be applicable to other industrial states such as New York, Massachusetts, and Michigan.

Four characteristics of the population by counties have been related to the strength of Democratic candidates during this period: the proportion of Roman Catholics in the total population;[34] the proportion of native-white persons of native parentage, thereby affording a converse measure of the proportion of persons of foreign background;[35] the proportion living on farms, hereinafter referred to as rural-farm population;[36] the proportion voting for repeal of the Eighteenth Amendment at the special election November 5, 1933.[37] The ten counties containing the highest percentage of Catholics, highest vote for repeal, lowest percentage of native white, and the highest percentage of rural-farm population, were listed in separate categories in order of rank. Generally speaking, the most urban counties are also preponderantly wet, Catholic and foreign.[38]

A comparison was made of the county's rank in Catholicity, rural-farm population, native-white population, and pro-repeal strength with its rank among the fifteen highest or lowest in vote returned for Democratic candidates in elections during the period 1928-1940. This comparison indicates: pronounced Democratic strength in the urban, foreign, Catholic, wet sections in 1928; an obliteration of this distinction in the 1932 election, bearing out the earlier hypothesis that the Roosevelt 1932 vote was largely a general protest vote against Hoover and not centered in any of the four social factors studied; beginning in 1934, an increasing proportion of Democratic strength came from the wet, foreign areas and the rural-farm population showed an increasing tendency to vote anti-Democratic.

A high degree of relationship was found between the 1928 Smith vote and Catholicity.[39] The Smith vote was closely related to the proportion of persons of foreign extraction, the proportion of city dwellers, and the ratio in favor of repeal of the Eighteenth Amendment in 1933.[40] A similar analysis of the Roosevelt vote in 1932 indicated the existence of the same relationship, but to a much lesser degree.[41] However, the vote for Roosevelt in 1936 reflected an increasing tendency of the Catholic and wet areas to support the New Deal candidates and the rural and non-foreign elements to oppose them.[42]

Virtually the same pattern of relationship was indicated in the vote for Governor Earle for United States senator in 1938.[43] No significant changes were discernible from the 1936 relationships, except with regard to rural-farm population, where a decrease in the magnitude of the inverse relationship were evident.[44] Since the 1940 election was closely related to those that preceded it, the same Democratic-Catholic-metropolitan-urban-foreign pattern was maintained.

The foregoing analyses may reasonably be interpreted as leading to the following general conclusions. During the period studied, the Catholic, foreign-born wet elements have tended to support the Democratic candidates, while the dry, rural voters have tended to turn against them; the exception was 1932, when the general protest vote against depression conditions tended to obliterate these particular relationships. Since 1932 the foregoing trend has become particularly noticeable, approaching in intensity the sharp social cleavages attending the 1928 campaign. The chief source of present Democratic strength in Pennsylvania is in the industrial areas and large centers of population.[45]

Party Tradition and Party Discipline, 1924-1940

Ideally, the strength of party tradition in a given state may be studied by interviewing a sample of citizens over a period of time and discovering to what extent they remained continuously loyal to given parties. Lacking the resources for such a survey, the extent to which the vote in given counties remained the same over a period of time was investigated.

A glance at Tables I, II, and III (see Appendix II) for the period 1924-1940 shows that, in spite of its reputation for loyalty to the Republican party, Pennsylvania has been noted for its independent voting. The tables show that the mean of the county Democratic percentages for President, during the period under discussion, varied from 25 per cent in 1924 to 52 per cent in 1936. Such a turnover might involve a shift of one-quarter of the voters. However, as we have seen, the increase in the Democratic percentage was in part the result of a rise in the general interest in voting. For the period under discussion, it might be assumed that three-quarters of the voters clung to their parties consistently.[46]

Pennsylvania has been the scene of many bitter factional quarrels. Before 1934 these quarrels were largely within the Republican party. Factional knifing of candidates is clearly shown in the 1930 election. The mean of the Democratic percentages for senator was only 29, but for governor it was 49. The difference may be attributed to the bitter opposition of the Vare faction in the Republican party to Gifford

Pinchot, the candidate of another faction for governor. Pinchot, twice governor of Pennsylvania, has been termed a Progressive due to his support of Theodore Roosevelt in 1912 and his opposition to the Vare machine, as well as his leadership in the conservation movement. However, comparison of the Pinchot vote in the Republican primaries of 1926, 1930 and 1934 with the LaFollette vote for president in 1924 and the Roosevelt vote in 1936, shows no relationship. The Pinchot strength was largely found in the rural areas, while that of LaFollette and the various New Deal candidates came from the urban centers.[47]

A comparison by counties of the Democratic percentages for different elections shows that there was a fairly close relationship between the 1928 and 1932 elections, but nothing like the striking similarity found for selected units in Chicago for the same elections.[48] After 1933 political alignments underwent a marked change in Pennsylvania. A Republican registration plurality of two million in 1932 shrank to 1,200,000 in 1934. A comparison of the vote for Earle for governor in 1934 and for Roosevelt in 1932 shows a somewhat closer relationship than that between Smith in 1928 and Roosevelt in 1932.[49] However, an even stronger resemblance was found between the Roosevelt 1936 vote and the Earle 1934 vote. In 1938, even though the Democrats lost and their mean county vote fell off by 10 per cent, the general pattern of that vote was closely modeled on the 1936 vote.[50] Two years later the third term issue did not prevent the Democratic mean county vote from rising again. Since the shifts were fairly uniform throughout the state, the county strength of the parties was not greatly changed.[51]

In addition to studying the strength of party tradition, it was also desirable to analyze party discipline. This was done by comparing the vote of candidates of the same party for different offices at the same election. Perfect party discipline would prevail if every citizen voted a straight ticket. In this study, consideration is limited to candidates for president, governor, and United States senator.

In 1928 the vote for Smith and the vote for McNair, Democratic candidate for United States senator, showed a fairly close relationship.[52] In 1932 party discipline was even higher, but in the 1934,

1936, 1938 and 1940 elections party discipline was almost perfect.[53] In spite of factional quarrels, it was stronger in Pennsylvania than in California, Illinois, Iowa or Wisconsin.[54]

Composite View

What is the relative importance of the different variables in explaining the politics of Pennsylvania? The situation is complex and it is almost impossible to disentangle the elements so that they can be weighed separately. A classification of counties showing the highest percentage vote for Democratic nominees for each election from 1924 to 1940 shows that the concentration of Democratic strength shifted .from certain rural sections prior to the New Deal to the industrial and mining areas subsequent to 1934.

Although the rural areas tended to vote anti-New Deal in the 1938 Earle election, they shifted less from the Democrats than did the urban areas between 1936 and 1938. The bulk of Earle's strength came from those who had supported Roosevelt in 1936 and party tradition was a strong influence. The voters who shifted least from the Democratic party lived in counties with high WPA rolls and a relatively high proportion of persons of foreign extraction.[55] Since the 1940 election was closely related to the 1938 and 1936 elections, the same generalizations would apply.

To summarize: Pennsylvania politics was fundamentally altered during the period 1928-1940. It will probably never revert to the industrial feudalism of the Penrose days. For better or worse, the miners and the textile workers have asserted themselves politically. A more even balance between the two major parties is to be expected than prevailed in the first quarter of the twentieth century. The new party alignment is rooted in economic differences, trade unionism, and a fundamental cleavage in political aims.

CHAPTER IV

PROGRESSIVE POLITICS: WISCONSIN

IN the north central and northwestern parts of the United States a distinct pattern of political behavior may be clearly noted.[1] When the nation swings in one direction, the states in this region move with it, but more strongly than the country as a whole. During the twenties these states—of which Wisconsin is typical—were more decidedly Republican than the nation, but during the thirties they became more strongly Democratic. This tendency to shift from one extreme to another is related to the progressive background of the region.[2]

"Wisconsin," "La Follette," "progressive"—these words have been for decades almost indissolubly linked in the minds of observers of the American political scene. Indeed, so strongly has the La Follette dynasty been identified with Wisconsin politics that the name "Wisfollette" has been bestowed on the state.[3] While Wisconsin has almost without exception followed the Republican standard in presidential elections from 1870 to 1932, it has shown progressive leanings. Its progressive tendencies appeared in the 1890's when the elder La Follette started to build a progressive faction within the Republican party, culminating in his election as governor in 1900 and United States Senator in 1906. The sulking of La Follette in 1912 greatly reduced the Progressive vote, but this vote was large enough to split the Republican vote and throw the state to Wilson. In 1924 Wisconsin overwhelmingly cast its vote for president for La Follette. Robert M. La Follette, Jr., succeeded his father as Senator in 1925.

Roosevelt carried Wisconsin in 1932 along with the other states in the progressive north central and northwestern bloc. Hanging on to his coattails were not only a Democratic senator, a Democratic governor, but a Democratic majority in the lower house of the Wisconsin legislature. Considering the weakness of the Democratic party in Wisconsin before 1932, this was truly a political revolution.[4]

Until 1934 the La Follette brothers, Robert M. and Philip, able tacticians, had as a rule followed the strategy of capturing the Republican primary nomination. They read into the party label meanings all their own. In 1934 the rift among Wisconsin Republicans between the stalwarts and the progressives, which had existed since the elder La Follette's early days, culminated in the launching of the Progressive party. Under its colors Robert M. La Follette was elected senator in 1934 and Philip La Follette governor in 1934 and 1936. By 1938 the political pendulum began to swing again in a conservative direction and the Republican party staged a spectacular comeback. However, Senator La Follette weathered the storms in 1940 although his running mate, Orland S. Loomis, lost the governorship to the Republican incumbent.[5]

What brought about this cyclical turn? As has been noted above, there is a tendency, not only in the United States, but in other democratic countries, for the opinions of voters to oscillate between progressive and non-progressive candidates. One explanation of these oscillations is that they are related to economic and social changes. In order to examine this theory in Wisconsin it is necessary to review briefly the economic characteristics of the state.

Following on the heels of the Wisconsin lumberjacks and miners came farmer-settlers. Drawn largely from northern European stock, they engaged at first in wheat farming, but after the 1890's they turned in increasing numbers to dairy farming. In the twentieth century there has been an increasing industrialization of the state, particularly in the southeastern area around Milwaukee. Although the state as a whole is now more urban than rural, and industry, service, and trade occupations are becoming increasingly important, these trends are confined to a relatively small part of the state.[6] The population in half of the 71 counties is more than 50 per cent rural-farm, and a little less than four-fifths of the counties have more than half their population living either on farms or in towns of less than 2,500 inhabitants. Hence, in analyzing voting behavior in Wisconsin by counties, agriculture's attitude in politics must engage our attention.

Between 1928 and 1932, the index number of Wisconsin farm prices dropped from 156 to 76, the lowest for the state in the last quarter century.[7] While the prices which the farmer paid for his clothes, feeds, and all other commodities also dropped between 1928 and 1932, the fall was not at all commensurate with the decline of farm prices. Thus the ratio of prices received to prices paid out by farmers fell from 102 in 1928 to 64 in 1932, a decrease of 37 per cent. At the same time, farm taxes were dropping much more slowly than cash income, resulting in an increasing, and in many cases an intolerable, tax burden. The cumulative effects of these conditions were increasing mortgaging of land and mortgage foreclosures, declining farm land values, and a gradual rise in tenancy.[8] There was, therefore, reason enough to expect the farmer to show his resentment against the party he had long supported but under whose administration he had suffered such economic disasters.

An examination of the 1932 returns for the various counties shows that there was no visible tendency as might have been expected for the farmers in the lowest-income areas to vote for Roosevelt and for those in the highest-income areas to vote for Hoover.[9] All farmers were apparently affected alike and the Roosevelt revolution was general. However, there was some relationship between the decrease in gross farm income during the years 1931-1933 and the shift to the Democratic party in the period 1928-1932.[10] In other words, there was a tendency toward greater shifts to Roosevelt in those areas with greater decreases in farm income.

A breakdown of the state into its socio-economic divisions sheds further light upon the situation.[11] These divisions show a great amount of homogeneity within themselves with reference to agricultural, social, and economic factors. Northern Wisconsin is the poorest section of the state. Known as the "cutover" area, it is a ghastly monument to the waste and destructiveness of the lumbering interests. Thousands of people were once employed in the mills and forests. When the timber supply was exhausted, they were left stranded to eke out a meagre living from the poor, stump-filled soils of the region. In 1929, the last year of "Republican prosperity," when the gross farm income per farm in the state averaged $2,250, the northeastern area averaged only $1,200, and the northwestern only $1,600.[12] The cutover region has the highest per cent tax delinquency in the state, the lowest value per farm of all products sold and used by the operator, the highest number of self-sufficing farms, the lowest per capita wealth in terms of property value, and the lowest ownership of such luxuries as radios, electric lights, bath tubs, and other gadgets regarded as essential to the American standard of living.[13] Certainly this area should have been expected to cast a protest vote against the party which had been so slow in getting a relief program under way. However, in 1932 the cutover region did not give Roosevelt a greater percentage of its vote than did the average county, nor did it shift more strongly to Roosevelt than did the rest of the state. Roosevelt's campaign promises in 1932 started no stampede. However, as is shown below, four years later the cutover counties were much more prone to take economic factors into consideration.

The only other section of the state comparable in poverty to the cutover region is the Central Sands area, a region of sandy soils, marshes, and wasteland. It can be divided into two parts, one of which has a much better grade of soil than the other. The poorest part[14] gave Roosevelt a comparatively high vote in 1932 and voted

strongly for the La Follettes. Contrasted with the poorest areas are the
prairie section and the southwest.[15] In the former, dairying and tobacco growing are the chief pursuits; the average farm income in
1929 was $3,000, and the standard of living is high; in the latter area
cheese and corn are the principal products. Both sections gave a relatively low vote to Roosevelt in 1932.

In contrast to the areas described above are the industrial sections
of the state—the heavily industrialized southeast and the less concentrated industrial areas of Lake Winnebago and the Michigan Lake
Shore.[16] Milwaukee, with its large working-class population, which
has for years shown Socialist leanings, went more strongly for Roosevelt than the state as a whole. While Norman Thomas had anticipat-
ed some of the elements of the New Deal program in the Socialist party
platform of 1932, Roosevelt stood a better chance of putting the short-
run planks into effect. The Lake-Shore-Winnebago area has both a
large farming and a large industrial population. The farming area
is one of the wealthiest in the state and a low Roosevelt vote might
have been expected here; but the region is also strongly Catholic and
it has been well established that the Catholics have Democratic leanings.[17] Roosevelt captured 69.6 per cent of the vote in the area, 2.6 per
cent more than in the state as a whole.

From the above analysis it is clear that the 1932 election was, in
general, a mass desertion of Herbert Hoover, who was associated in the
minds of the voters with the depression.

Between 1933 and 1936, the economic trends of the 1929-1932 period were reversed for Wisconsin. The farm price index rose 76 per
cent from a low of 67 to 118—the latter almost equal to the 1930
figure. On the other hand, the cost of the materials which farmers
bought rose only 20 per cent. As a result, the ratio of prices received
to prices paid rose 47 per cent from over the 1932 figure. The Wisconsin farmer was therefore, so far as buying was concerned. almost as
well off in 1936 as in the twenties and early thirties. While the New
Deal propagandists tried to take advantage of this situation, Roosevelt lost votes in 1936 in many agricultural areas and maintained his

state ratio only because of his increased popularity in highly industrialized areas.

In trying to understand the 1936 Wisconsin vote it must be remembered that much of the state's agriculture centers around dairying and that the dairy industry refused to join the AAA program. The total farm benefits paid in Wisconsin from 1933 to 1936 amounted to only $16,000,000, while the total farm income for the same period was $556,000,000. AAA checks were "small potatoes" in this state and those farmers who were paid for plowing under wheat, tobacco, and corn did not show any great loyalty to the apostle of farm scarcity.[18]

The tariff policies of Secretary Cordell Hull apparently concerned the welfare of the Wisconsin farmers much more directly than the AAA. In January, 1936, the reciprocal trade treaty with Canada went into effect; among other things it lowered the duty on dairy cattle and on Canadian cheddar (American) cheese. These concessions were seized upon by the Republicans as a good issue with which to stir up the Wisconsin farmers' resentment against the New Deal. The issue was stressed by both John Hamilton, Republican campaign manager, and George Peek, a former New Dealer.[19] Governor Alf Landon, the Republican presidential candidate, also made a special bid for the dairy farmers' votes.[20] He cited lower cheese prices and greatly increased imports of Canadian cheese as evidence of how the New Deal policies had injured the dairy farmer. Since dairying, of which cheesemaking is an important part, is the leading industry in Wisconsin in the value of its products,[21] and since American cheese constitutes 75 per cent of Wisconsin cheese production, these charges, if true, might have had serious repercussions in the state's vote in 1936. The cheese issue was regarded as serious enough to bring replies from Hull, Secretary of Agriculture Henry A. Wallace, and the President himself. Newspapers[22] differed sharply in their estimates of the strength of the Republican propaganda.[23] The defenders of the program pointed out that the decline in cheese prices was a regular seasonal one and that prices for the year as a whole showed an advance over the preceding years.[24] Cheese production in 1936 was surpassed only by that of 1925 and milk production was the highest on record. With prices of dairy products rising and the cost of living lagging behind, the farmer could certainly not rationally complain about the tariff issue.

It is striking, therefore, that the southwestern, the Lake Shore, and the north central areas, which are the leading producers of American and other cheeses, all showed decreases in 1936 of about 5 per cent from the 1932 vote for Roosevelt, although the average county had a decrease of only 2.5 per cent. Of the leading cheese producing counties, the five which are over 75 per cent rural (farm and non-farm) averaged an 8.4 per cent decrease from 1932. The record of the voting shift, then, would favor the theory that the reciprocal trade treaty propaganda exerted some influence. The maps (Figures 7, 8, and 9) on the following pages give the pattern of political behavior in the state.

The analysis of the 1936 vote on the basis of the agricultural-economic division of the state tends to show that there was a definite relationship between economic status and Roosevelt's popularity, except in the middle income areas. Roosevelt was no longer an unknown quantity. His New Deal had alienated certain economic sectors of the population and attracted others. A comparison of the rank order of the different agricultural sections in per cent for the New Deal with the rank order in farm income brings this out clearly.

If we omit the prairie section, which because of several large cities can be only doubtfully classified as rural, and which, moreover, contains Madison, the state capital and a La Follette stronghold, there is a close correspondence between economic conditions and the rural vote for president. Thus the northern cutover areas gave 70, 70 and 66 per cent for Roosevelt. On the other hand, the wealthier rich Central Sands, Western Wheat, and southwestern areas, listed in order of increasing average farm income per farm, gave the president 61, 57 and 55 per cent (respectively) of their votes.

The period from the latter part of 1937 until November, 1938, marked a sharp recession in economic conditions. The farm price index for Wisconsin dropped from 125 to 103 (18 per cent) during this one year and the farmer's purchasing power fell from 93 to 82—

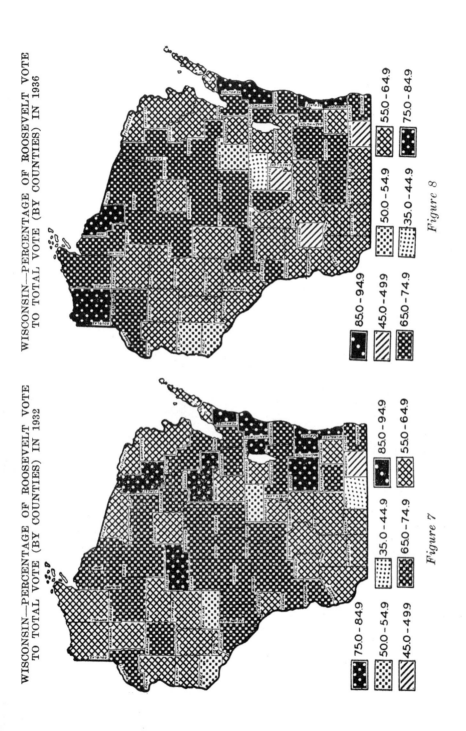

WISCONSIN—PERCENTAGE OF ROOSEVELT VOTE
TO TOTAL VOTE (BY COUNTIES) IN 1936

85.0 - 94.9   50.0 - 54.9   55.0 - 64.9

45.0 - 49.9   35.0 - 44.9

65.0 - 74.9   75.0 - 84.9

Figure 8

WISCONSIN—PERCENTAGE OF ROOSEVELT VOTE
TO TOTAL VOTE (BY COUNTIES) IN 1932

75.0 - 84.9   35.0 - 44.9   85.0 - 94.9

50.0 - 54.9   55.0 - 64.9

45.0 - 49.9   65.0 - 74.9

Figure 7

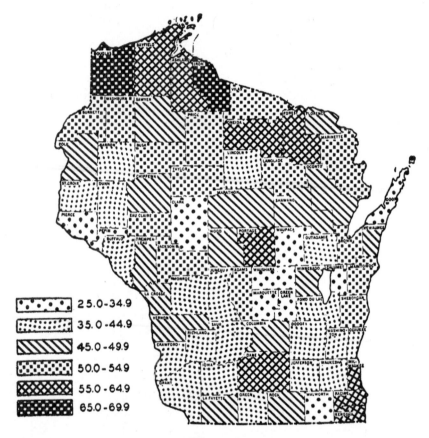

Figure 9

a decline of 12 per cent. Wisconsin industrial conditions showed a similar trend—the index of employment[25] fell 17 per cent and that for pay rolls 22 per cent. The contraction seems to have especially affected the industrial population. With the exception of the northern cutover region, the greatest increases in relief cases during this period were recorded in the large urban industrial areas. Some of the wealthier rural counties even showed a decrease in percentage on relief.[26]

This industrial depression seems to have been partially reflected in Wisconsin voting in 1938. So far as could be learned, the principal plank in the platform of John P. Heil, the Republican gubernatorial candidate, was economy and this offered a potential threat to the unemployed.[27] A definite relationship was found between the Republican vote and various measures of economic status. In general, the lower the economic status and the more dependent the voters in a given county upon government aid, the lower was the vote for Heil. However, he won the election.

The agricultural-economic sectional analysis corroborates the findings by counties. Using the word "unemployed" to mean totally unemployed and emergency workers, the percentages unemployed (1937) of the total gainfully employed (1930) were compared by sections. The comparison revealed that, except for the deviation of two sections—the western wheat and Lake Shore-Winnebago areas—a one-to-one inverse correlation exists between the rank order of the sections as to unemployment and their order in per cent vote for Heil. A similar state of affairs existed in the eight predominantly agricultural sections with reference to rankings by average gross farm income per farm. Except for a slight shift in the rankings of the north central and western wheat areas, the richer the farms of a given section, the higher was the vote for Heil.

President Roosevelt carried Wisconsin in 1940 but his margin was extremely close and his average losses by counties (17 per cent) were greater than in any other of the states studied. The average shift away from Roosevelt in the Wisconsin counties was more than three times that found in the Pennsylvania counties. Where were these huge New Deal losses concentrated and what economic reasons may be advanced to explain them? Roosevelt's popularity declined most in the industrial and rich farming Lake Shore-Winnebago regions, and least in the cutover areas and in certain southern urban centers such as Janesville and Madison. In part these shifts (1936-1940) were a reflection of the forces which elected Republican Governor Heil in 1938. However, Heil's 1940 vote was considerably less than his 1938 vote throughout the state. It is clear that the national New Deal policies had a strong appeal to certain Wisconsin voters and that they reversed trends which were indicated in the state election returns.

In general, it would appear that economic motivations were important in accounting for the high shift to Democratic candidates in 1932, but variations in the vote were not related to variations in economic status. By 1936 this picture had changed to a great extent, and there were definite indications of an "economic" vote. This economic consciousness continued to grow with the recurrence of a sharp recession or depression and in the 1938 gubernatorial election it was, apparently, a leading factor in accounting for the election of Heil and the defeat of Philip La Follette.

Closely related to purely economic considerations is the degree of urbanization.[28] How are the differences in attitudes between farmers, small town and city dwellers reflected in their political behavior?[29] An examination of the detailed returns reveals a tendency for the farming areas to be more strongly Republican and conservative than the more urban counties. This tendency was not, it seems, very strong in 1932, but after four years of the New Deal the anti-Roosevelt bias of the rural areas became more pronounced.

The relation of the degree of urbanization to Wisconsin progressivism is not so clear.[30] A study based on the separation of rural-farm and non-rural-farm population conceals more than it reveals, for the latter category includes people living in towns of many sizes, from under 2,500 to metropolitan centers like Milwaukee. To obtain a more refined approach to the problem, the population of the state was divided into five sections—the city of Milwaukee; cities over 25,-000 except Milwaukee; cities of 10,000 to 25,000; cities of 2,500 to

10,000; and areas under 2,500. The votes in each were then tabulated and converted into percentages. In 1932 the rural population was exceeded only by the city of Milwaukee in its anti-Hooverism, and it was the small urban areas[31] which gave Roosevelt his lowest vote. In 1936, the trend of the rural vote was away from the New Deal. All three of the larger urban groupings showed gains of five or six per cent in the vote for Roosevelt; the small towns showed no changes, and the rural areas showed a loss of 4 per cent. Although the farmer's condition had been improved in 1936, he tended to return to his older political habits to some extent. Wisconsin farmers, receiving little in the way of corn, wheat, tobacco, and cotton benefits, thought that most of the New Deal gains in Wisconsin were obtained by the urban dweller.

The reaction of the city dweller to the New Deal was in sharp contrast to that of the rural citizen. Of the twenty-seven cities in Wisconsin with over 10,000 population, only two failed to show a gain for Roosevelt in 1936 and six showed gains of over 10 per cent. The largest city—Milwaukee—with 20 per cent of the state's population, was also the most strongly pro-New Deal of any of the five sectors. In fact, with 83 per cent of its total Republican and Democratic vote going to Roosevelt in 1936, it was the most pro-New Deal large city in the country outside of the South; and several large Milwaukee suburbs, notably West Allis with 87 per cent Democratic, and Cudahy with 90 per cent, compared favorably with most southern cities. This metropolitan center is especially interesting because of its Socialist strength. In 1932 almost 13 per cent of the total vote had gone to the Socialist presidential candidate, with 19 per cent for Hoover, and 67 per cent for Roosevelt; in 1936 only two per cent and in 1940 only one per cent still remained Socialist. In the reaction against Socialism, Roosevelt gained; the Republicans lost; and in 1936 a new party, the Union Party, sponsored by Father Charles E. Coughlin, received 5 per cent of the total vote. What seems to have happened is this: the Socialists felt that Roosevelt's policies corresponded sufficiently with their own short run aims to merit their support.

The rural-urban analysis of the gubernatorial elections indicates even more strongly a divergence between rural and urban behavior or, more precisely, between the rural and the small urban areas. In the 1932 Republican primary election and the gubernatorial elections for 1934 and 1936, La Follette received 54, 47 and 50 per cent, respectively, of the total rural vote; on the other hand, the cities between 2,500 and 25,000 population gave La Follette 33, 33 and about 40 per cent of the total vote for these same elections—a difference of 10 per cent or more in each of the three elections.

In general, the people in the smaller Wisconsin cities and towns are the most conservative in the state. The rural population is the most progressive, although it was not the most pro-New Deal in the 1930 decade. The citizens of Milwaukee and other large cities of over 25,000 were strongly Democratic and New Deal during this period in both national and state politics, but not nearly as progressive as the ruralites until the 1936 election. Although the data are unfortunately not available for 1938, the figures for Milwaukee County would tend to support the thesis that Milwaukee had receded from its brief period of progressivism. In 1940 Milwaukee County was still strong Roosevelt territory, but the decrease in the President's popularity was just as great here as in other parts of the state.

Since 51 per cent of Wisconsin's population is foreign born or of foreign parentage, the relation of nativity to voting has significance.[32] The figures for 1936 show a definite tendency for areas of high foreign population to vote strongly for Roosevelt, although this was not clear in 1932. It is likely that the foreign voters flocked to Roosevelt because of economic considerations rather than for reasons connected with their origin.[33] The foreigners in Wisconsin are concentrated, for the most part, in the northern cutover area, with a lesser concentration in the southeastern industrial region. Since these are the areas in which the people suffered the greatest economic deprivation during the depression and in which the New Deal distributed its greatest largess in the way of relief grants, it was to be expected that the citizens, whether or not of foreign nativity, should show their gratitude.[34]

The 1938 gubernatorial election brought out more strongly the tendency for the foreign group to vote against conservative Republican candidates.[35] However, the importance of this factor is not clear since Heil received his lowest votes in the most economically depressed sectors of the state—which were, for the most part, also highly foreign. On the other hand, there seems to be a definite relationship between foreignness and progressivism, irrespective of economic conditions. The average per cent native white for the fifteen traditionally strong progressive counties was 46.7 per cent, while the votes for the Republican and Democratic parties in these regions in 1938 were, respectively, 57 and 56.2 per cent. Moreover, there was a difference in the nationality makeups of these groups of counties. The Democratic group was overwhelmingly German with a few Czechoslovakian and Polish areas. The stalwart Republican groups had much more Scandinavian composition but were still predominantly German. Most of the progressive counties, on the other hand, were predominantly Scandinavian, although there was a large German group also. The tie between progressivism and the Scandinavians goes far back into the state's history. The elder La Follette derived his most substantial support from the Wisconsin Norwegians at the beginning of the progressive movement.[36] Regardless of the reasons why this first occurred, the Scandinavian group seems to have remained predominantly progressive ever since.

The economic and social milieu is seen to have played some part in the Wisconsin elections of the thirties, especially in the latter part of the decade, but in our American election system with its highly organized parties the purely political or organizational influences should also be considered. Of these, party discipline and party tradition may be defined in operational terms. Party discipline refers ideally to the success of a given party in obtaining support for all its candidates, state and national. This study, however, is limited to presidential, senatorial and gubernatorial candidates. If there is a one-to-one correlation between the votes for governor and for president, it may be said that party discipline is perfect. That is, for every vote cast for the state candidates one was cast for the national candidate.[37] Many influences may lead to divergence, i.e., weak party discipline.

The two candidates, although members of the same party, may have different policies or personal appeal; or one candidate may get more votes than the other because of the prominence of his office, interest in the election, position on the ballot, or any number of other considerations. In Wisconsin, the situation has been especially complicated by the nominal existence of only two major parties before 1934 and of a tripartite setup thereafter. Hence, in considering party discipline for the period 1924-40, it is best to examine two periods—that of 1924-32 and 1934-40.

The facts reveal a consistently high party discipline in the ''regular'' Republican party—a discipline which existed even when the La Follettes controlled the party. This was shown by the two elections between 1924 and 1934, in which the regular Republicans managed to wrest control from the La Follettes.[38] Since 1934, when the La Follette faction abandoned the Republican party, the Republicans have exhibited a higher discipline than in previous years. The strong differences existing between the two elements which formerly made up the Wisconsin Republican party is further shown by examining the votes of La Follette Republicans and those of regular Republicans.[39] Here there was a consistently inverse or low positive relationship between candidates ostensibly belonging to the same party—additional evidence that the present tripartite division was a reality even before the progressives decided to form a separate party. Before 1934 the Progressives did not exhibit a very high discipline although the party organizational tendency was noticeable.[40] Since 1934, there has been high discipline. This is especially true of the relationship between the supporters of the La Follette brothers in 1934.

A review of the data on Democratic party discipline shows that despite the fact that the Democrats for years were unable to win an election, they managed to maintain a rather high discipline. When their chance came in 1932, there was already the nucleus of a strong state organization which could be put to good use. The previous analysis furnishes a general overview of party discipline, but it does not bring out clearly the importance of discipline or lack of it at the specific elections. In the 1932 election the Democratic discipline was higher than that achieved by any other party, and was in fact the highest that any of the parties had reached in a decade.[41] This strong organization was probably one of the principal factors in electing a Democratic senator, a Democratic governor and Democratic presidential electors. The fact that the Democratic senatorial candidate polled less votes than Roosevelt, and the Democratic governor less than the senator, would further suggest that the powerful national organization pulled the state organization to victory.

In 1936 the vote for Alexander Wiley, the Republican gubernatorial candidate, was very closely related to that for Landon, G.O.P. candidate for president. On the other hand, neither Democratic nor Progressive votes for governor showed any significant relation to Roosevelt's votes in the different counties. However, it is probable that the people who voted Progressive or Democratic locally also voted for Roosevelt.[42] Another fact tending to lend credence to this view is that Bob La Follette, as in 1932, endorsed Roosevelt and probably carried many Progressive followers with him.[43] The 1936 split in the parties was a split largely between the Democrats and the Progressives.

In the 1938 election, the Republican candidates for governor and senator, Heil and Wiley, respectively, were victorious. The winning party showed the highest discipline and the Democrats the lowest.[44] What had happened to lower the discipline of the Democratic organization within two years and to encompass the defeat of Philip La Follette? A glance at the 1938 primary provides a partial explanation.

R. K. Henry, a conservative Democrat, whose avowed objective was to defeat La Follette, ran in both the Republican and the Democratic gubernatorial primaries. He succeeded in capturing the Democratic nomination and was second to Heil, the winner, in the Republican primaries, with a combined vote exceeding that received by any other entrant. Henry's vote, in fact, was at least twice that of any of the candidates except Phil La Follette and Heil. Therefore, when Henry failed to receive the nominations of both parties opposing La Follette, he withdrew and threw his strength to Heil, the Republican nominee. The Democratic State Committee then hurriedly put up a make-shift candidate—seventy-four year old Bolens. He received less than half the votes cast for Democratic aspirants for office in the primaries, only the most rock-ribbed of Democrats adhering to the party banner.

It is difficult to show with any degree of accuracy just what happened to the votes lost by the Democrats. It would seem reasonable, *a priori,* to suppose that Henry's votes went to Heil. Those who had voted for Henry in the Democratic primary were probably strongly anti-La Follette and therefore switched to Heil. Several quantitative measures tend to bear out this hypothesis.[45] A regional analysis of Henry's votes indicates that he tended to draw his strength from urban areas containing native white, wealthy farm elements and few people on relief.[46] These are the same sections from which Heil derived his votes and the opposite which formed the backbone of Phil La Follette's constituents. There is, clearly, a strong indication that the Henry vote went predominantly to Heil. Economic and social considerations were able to break through the organizational lines established in the four preceding years in the Democratic party, and badly disrupt party discipline. Henry's defection from Democratic ranks was probably an important element in the Republican victory in 1938.

The 1940 election furnishes one of the best illustrations of the fluidity of party lines in Wisconsin. The voters showed their independence of party lines by choosing a Democrat for president, a Progressive for United States senator, and a Republican for governor. There was a fairly high inverse relationship between the votes for Roosevelt and Heil, indicating that Roosevelt drew upon Democratic and Progressive elements. An examination of the ballots would probably show that Roosevelt got nearly all the Progressive votes, that there was a handful of straight ticket Democratic voters, and that at least 40 per cent of the voters were loyal to the Republican slate of Willkie and Heil. Democratic state candidates were unable to ride to power on Roosevelt's coattails as in 1932. The Republicans won the governorship by a narrow margin, but they could not dislodge the popular Bob La Follette from the United States Senate.

The other political measure selected for examination is that of party tradition—the ability of a party to hold on to its constituency over a period of time. If a party succeeds in persuading the same areas to give the same percentage of votes to its candidates in a series of elections, we say it has high party tradition.

An analysis of these data by scatter diagrams shows that party tradition was not strong in Wisconsin, although the Democrats maintained a fairly high tradition during the New Deal, especially in presidential elections. In state elections party lines were more consistent than one would expect from comparing state and national results in any one election. A Democratic candidate for governor is likely to obtain support from the same sections of the state whether he runs in a presidential year or not.[47]

Although the above technique does not show a high partisan voting tradition, a county by county analysis reveals certain areas with traditional partisan fixations. Eight elections of the last decade were analyzed for country votes for each of the three parties. The Democratic area is concentrated in the eastern tier of counties along Lake Michigan and Lake Winnebago. This includes most of the populous counties.[48] As compared with the other two traditionally partisan areas, the average county in the Democratic group contains the wealthiest farming element, but this element is far less important than in the Republican or Progressive counties. In fact, many Democratic counties are predominantly urban—including Milwaukee. Despite the presence of a large urban working class, the percentage on relief in this sector is less than in the other two sectors. By far the greatest proportions of Catholics and pro-repeal elements are in the traditionally Democratic counties.[49]

In strong contrast are the Progressive counties,[50] comprising for the most part the northern cutover and poor central sands districts and the southern part of the western wheat area adjoining the poor central sands district. These areas—60 per cent rural farm as compared to 40 per cent in the Democratic sectors—on the average contain the poorest farmers of the state. They averaged $1,250 income per farm in 1936, compared with $2,000 in the Democratic sector.

Moreover, 21 per cent of the population in the Progressive sectors was receiving some form of public assistance in 1938, and 25 per cent of the gainfully employable were unemployed. By all odds, then, these traditionally Progressive counties contain the most economically depressed populations. The latter also are, relatively speaking, in favor of prohibition, are much more foreign than either the Republican or Democratic populations and contain relatively few Catholics. The backbone of Wisconsin progressivism of the last decade was, then, the poor Protestant farmers badly hit by the depression.

The traditional stalwart Republican counties are scattered over the state.[51] Their characteristics are for the most part intermediate between the extremes shown by the Democratic and Progressive counties. In economic characteristics they are quite similar to the Democratic segments of the population, although not quite as well off. In their social characteristics they tend to resemble the Progressive areas, being predominantly rural, although containing several large cities, a low percentage Catholics, even less for repeal than are the Progressives, but containing greater proportions of native white population than the other groups. The separation between the two wings of the Republican party before 1934 would seem to lie mainly in their economic differentials, with the factors of smaller foreign and greater urban populations as secondary characteristics.

Summary

From the data available precise generalizations are risky. However, certain tentative conclusions do seem justifiable. The depression appears to have worked toward a political realignment of the socio-economic groupings in Wisconsin. It began with a wholesale political turnover in 1932, in which every section of the population took part, the "scapegoat" factor probably being the most important. The poor, traditionally Progressive areas showed the greatest shifts between 1928 and 1932, but the heaviest Democratic votes were recorded in relatively wealthy parts of the state where traditional political alignments plus other non-economic factors such as Catholicism and anti-prohibition were of prime import. By 1936 new lines were beginning to be delineated, although hazily. The New Deal gained strength among the poor, foreign, progressive farmers of the northern cutover area, and in the large cities with their great number of skilled and unskilled laborers and high relief loads. Progressive farmers, accustomed to voting the Republican ticket both locally and nationally prior to 1932 and 1934, followed their leaders, the La Follettes, in forsaking the Republican standard for the Democratic New Deal. Similarly the large Socialist element among the workers of the Milwaukee metropolitan area voted almost completely for the party whose leader had incorporated into his own policies some items from the short-run program of the Socialists.

The 1938 election, although witnessing a reaction against the Progressive party whose support had been one of the principal elements of 1936 New Deal strength in Wisconsin, showed in more striking fashion the tendency for economic and other non-political forces to change the habitual forms of political behavior. The defection of a conservative Democratic leader was the precipitating factor leading to a wholesale desertion by Democrats to the anti-Progressive Republican candidate. It is probable that in 1938 and 1940 the elements which deserted the Democratic party were the more economically affluent native white people, similar to those who had been the mainstay of the Republican organization during the thirties.

In Wisconsin, then, the realignment of the population along more "realistic" lines, long called for by many students of the American party system, seems to have been realized as a result of the economic hardships of the thirties. This trend, however, is strongly conditioned by religious and ethnic factors, and especially by the lag of traditional voting habits.

CHAPTER V

FARM BELT POLITICS: IOWA

AN EXAMINATION of the election returns for Iowa before 1932 might lead to the conclusion that its citizens had a strong Republican fixation which made them impervious to the more general shifts in the political fortunes of the two major parties. But a closer view shows that during the past forty years the state has been exceedingly sensitive to political and social changes. The late Senator J. P. Dolliver was commonly credited with the statement: "Iowa will go Democratic in the year that Hell goes Methodist." From 1864 to 1932 only two Democratic candidates broke the Republican tradition: Horace Boies, who served two terms as governor during the Populist era, and Daniel Steck, who was seated by the Senate in 1925 in place of Smith W. Brookhart despite the fact that the latter had received a certificate of election from the state. In 1924 Steck, the Democratic candidate, was given the support of the Republican organization which was determined to punish Brookhart for his insurgency.

It is true that before the New Deal era, Democratic candidates were only successful in state-wide elections under extraordinary conditions;[1] but when the country began to shift toward the Democratic party the state went a little farther in that direction than the nation as a whole.[2] Of all the states showing this tendency, Iowa was the least flexible. It thus lies between the extremely flexible states and those that parallel national trends closely.

As in other prairie states, agriculture has been declining in economic importance in Iowa, but it is still the state's most fundamental activity. It absorbs one-third of the gainfully employed, and the gross farm income constitutes a large part of the state's purchasing power.[3] The prosperity of the businessmen, professionals, and in general the "white collar" workers who serve the farmers is directly dependent upon income from farming.[4] Since agriculture occupies a central position in the economic life of the state, it is important to examine its structure in pre- and post-depression years, and then to attempt to relate various differential aspects within the state to variations in the popular vote for president.

A study by T. W. Schultz of Iowa State College, covering the period 1925 to 1935, is especially helpful in revealing Iowa's agriculture structure.[5] He chose the years 1925 to 1929 as the base 100, and 1932-33 as the depth of the depression.[6] In the period 1925-1935 the cash income of Iowa farmers was derived as follows: four-fifths from the sale of livestock (chiefly hogs) and one-fifth from the sale of crops (chiefly corn), except that in 1935 "benefit payments" under the AAA were sizable (11.4 per cent). This income is, of course, determined by both the amount produced and the price received per unit.[7] Except for certain irregular forces, such as insects and droughts, the amount produced steadily increased because of the rise in efficiency of production; hence, price is the key to the fluctuations in total income. The fact that the price index went lower than the income index during the depression and higher in

1935 resulted from the nature of farm production on the down-curve of the depression cycle and from the curtailment in total supply due to AAA and the 1934 drought.

The *Iowa Yearbook of Agriculture* for 1939 contains a number of studies similar to Schultz's for 1925-1935. During the period 1935 to 1939, Iowa cash farm income continued to be derived from the same three principal sources—crops, livestock, and government payments.[8] Government payments dropped after 1935 but rose again in 1939. Prices received for farm products fell in 1938 and 1939, but the total cash farm income rose because of rising total production.

Production of farm produce is carried on by a great number of individuals competing with each other for the national market and for the declining world market. Each farmer's supply is an insignificant portion of the total product, and hence, has a negligible effect on the price. Thus, the individual farmer's income is a function only of the amount he produces, which in turn depends upon his diligence and efficiency. However, if all farmers increase production the total supply will rise and thus tend to lower prices. The demand for foods is relatively inelastic; hence, an increase in supply produces a disproportionate decline in prices and thus a loss in total revenue. It is precisely in the difference between the farmer as an individual producer and as a collective producer that his dilemma arises. Herein may be found the explanation of why the price index falls below the income index. Thus, after 1929, when the purchasing power of the urban population declined rapidly, agricultural prices spiralled downward along with other prices; but each farmer, viewing only his own rather than the total situation, strove the harder to maintain his income by producing more in order to meet his relatively rigid expenses. In this way, of course, he only made matters worse. This is substantiated by such facts as the definite relation between income during the depression and increased erosion due to overworking the soil.[9]

More important than cash income in measuring economic welfare is real income, *i.e.*, the relation of the farmer's cash income to his expenses. The most significant expenditures are those for production, living, taxes, and interest on borrowed capital. Schultz's analysis shows that the first two—production and living expenses—did not fall as fast as price, but recovered more rapidly. Property taxes were slowly being reduced, but still represented a heavy burden on the farmer; interest on borrowed capital also did not fall in proportion to income. Furthermore, with respect to the farmer's capital structure, the value of farm land and buildings fell tremendously, especially in the period 1930 to 1935.[10] So great was this disparity between cash income and real income that by 1932 the farmer's plight had become well-nigh unbearable. He was losing his farm at a time when his industry and skill had yielded him maximum production. Farm tenancy, slowly creeping upon him in the prewar days, rapidly deprived him of his traditional independence in the depression years following 1929. In 1890 only 28 per cent of Iowa farms were operated by tenants, but by 1935 over 50 per cent were operated in this manner. Not only had the proportion of owner-operated farms dropped, but fewer owners were reaching the mortgage-free stage.[11] Small wonder that there was considerable discontent in 1932. As Dr. John Black said in the beginning of that year, "There is imminent danger that Iowa will harvest this fall the biggest crop of farm mortgage closures, lost equities, and ruined farmers the state has ever known."[12] Farm strikes, mob violence, and a huge Democratic vote were among the signs of the time. Hoover became a scapegoat for the personal insecurity of many Iowa farmers.

The magnitude of the Republican upset in 1932 is revealed by an analysis of political trends in the state during the years 1924-1940.[13] The weakness of the Democratic party before the depression is clearly shown by the lack of interest in the Democratic primaries, by the absence of Democratic congressmen, and by the overwhelming Republican character of the state legislature. While the 1930 elections brought success to one Democratic candidate for Congress and to an unusually large number of Democratic candidates for the state legislature, it was not until 1932 that the Democratic tide was in full swing.   In this particular, Iowa followed national trends. Roosevelt received 21 per cent more of the 1932 vote cast in Iowa than Al Smith did of the 1928 vote.   The voters in large numbers all over the state overcame the inertia of seventy years of Republicanism and, in their despair at the economic ruin which had engulfed their once prosperous state, they turned to the prophet of the New Deal.

The national administration under Roosevelt envisaged a solution of the agricultural problem in two ways: slashing tariffs, and/or cutting total agricultural production.[14]   Since the tariffs could be lowered only gradually and the plight of the farmer was immediately pressing, the AAA was put into operation.   It lasted from 1934 to 1936, when it was declared unconstitutional by the Supreme Court. Shortly after this legal setback Congress passed the Soil Conservation and Domestic Allotment Act but it failed to solve the problems of undersupply caused by the drought and over-supply caused by huge agricultural surpluses.   The Agricultural Adjustment Act of 1938 provided a reserve to take care of the short crop years, and at the same time it endeavored to maintain prices in the bountiful crop years by means of the Commodity Loan Program.   This so-called "Ever-Normal Granary" plan was apparently well received by Iowa farmers.[15]   The effect of these agricultural policies upon Roosevelt's political fortunes in Iowa must be viewed in relation to the economic and social characteristics of the various sections of the state.

Roosevelt suffered the most pronounced losses in 1936 as compared with 1932 in the southern pasture[16] and the western meat areas, while he held his ground and even gained in the cash grain area.[17]   From the long-run point of view the southern pasture area ranks lowest in economic welfare, as is indicated by the distribution of annual per capita real income, distribution of "farm home conveniences,"[18] land and building values,[19] average annual corn yields, and shipment of corn.[20]   On the other hand, the northern cash grain area is most prosperous, the western meat area, the east central meat area, and the dairy area intermediate in the order given.   The southern part of the state also has the greatest proportions of native white population and older people,[21] whereas the northern part has the lowest proportions. There is an apparent contradiction in the above dichotomy of the state with respect to the decline of farmer independence, from owner to mortgagee, to tenant, to farm laborer, since a greater percentage of mortgages is found in the northern cash grain area[22] than in the southern area. But this is probably due to the fact that the wealthier farm areas are the first to be most heavily mortgaged.[23]

With reference to short-run trends two outstanding events drastically disrupted the economic structure of Iowa—the droughts of 1934 and 1936. The first drought, covering especially 32 southern counties, was regarded as the most severe in Iowa history.[24] The drought of 1936 is even more important, for it immediately preceded the presidential election and affected most severely the southern pasture and the western meat areas—the regions shifting most decidedly against Roosevelt.[25] Even if Roosevelt had not inaugurated a farm program, farmers hit hardest by the drought would have tended to vote against him in protest. However, the AAA, instituted as a means of curtailing the corn-hog supply in order to raise prices for the farmers, accentuated the drought hardships in a totally unforeseen manner.

The entire state raises corn mainly for livestock feed. However, the southern area (and the dairy area) produces barely enough to feed its livestock in normal years whereas the cash grain area ships a considerable surplus. The AAA plus the drought (especially in 1936) so reduced the total supply of corn that its price rose to new highs.[26] The rest of the state and especially the southern pasture and the western meat areas had such a relatively low corn production that not only were they unable to take advantage of the rise in corn prices but they had to buy corn for feed from the cash grain area. Thus, actually the northern cash grain area benefited under the AAA and the drought at the expense of the western and southern counties, and, to a lesser extent, of the dairy and east central meat areas.

The drought conditions of 1935 and 1936 left lasting political scars on the areas most directly affected. In 1940 the western meat area, once a Democratic stronghold, shifted most violently against the New Deal. The cash grain area shifted only slightly away from Roosevelt. A *New York Times* correspondent on November 10, 1940, explained the effect of the drought on voting behavior as follows:

> In spite of all the grants, loans and payments, in spite of the whole business, farmers have been having mighty tough times. So they went to the polls Tuesday and voted against tough times. They weren't voting against Mr. Roosevelt or for Mr. Willkie so much. They were just voting against seven years of drought. They wanted a change.
>
> If that wasn't it, then why was the drought area the only large block of states in the nation that went solid for Willkie?[27]

The preceding section of this chapter has dealt primarily with historical and descriptive economic material in order to give the background for a more precise quantitative formulation of political trends. In the highly urbanized areas of the United States the voting in the 1936 election was clearly along class lines—salaried groups supported Landon and the wage earning proletariat supported Roosevelt, with the "white collar" lower middle class holding the balance of power. In Iowa, the farm element was the decisive factor. Thus, in searching for an economic index representative of the entire state, it was decided that the economic relations of the farmer would be given most weight.[28]

In approaching the problem of selecting the proper unit for comparing the distribution of votes with the distribution of economic satisfaction, it was necessary to keep in mind the nature of the vote and the manner in which it and other social and economic data are reported.[29] The 99 Iowa counties were selected chiefly because election, social, economic data are recorded mainly for these units. However, certain limitations must be observed.[30] Although many of the counties are homogeneous, a significant number are not. Thus, 16 are over 50 per cent urban in population. Besides the different socio-economic structure in the cities, the agricultural areas themselves differed notably, as discussed above. These factors tend to weaken the presumption of a connection between the predominant vote and the predominant social or economic characteristic. Since the vote by county is simply the undifferentiated gross of all the various groups within the county, we may presume that the predominant shift in the vote from 1932 to 1936 and from 1936 to 1940 was associated with the predominant economic or social characteristics.

Economic indexes can, in general, be separated into long-run and short-run types. The former is represented by such indexes as value of land and buildings per farm, average value of land per acre, and productivity of land per acre; these are usually quite stable over a period of years.[31] For the short run type, income for the year seems most appropriate.[32] In fact, the two aspects of income may be said to embrace the entire concept of the economic index. The short-run income can be viewed as generalized purchasing power secured by the farmer through the production and sale of his produce, i.e., his cash income = amount of produce $\times$ price per unit. The long-run income can be viewed as the conversion of the generalized purchasing power (money) into specific items of utility ranging from food and clothing to land and buildings. The particular commodities into which the farmer converts his money depend upon the marginal utility of his money in relation to the utility of the commodities bought. Between the two general types of income it would seem that cash income would be most useful for correlation with vote distributions because (1) generalized purchasing power must be obtained before it can be converted into specific items of use; (2) the amount of income determines the marginal utility of the farmer's money and hence the latitude of his choice; (3) each individual consumer has a special utility scale and hence the range of choices between commodities covering the same need becomes very great; and finally (4), the shifts in the popular support of candidates and parties are becoming much more sudden.[33] It may be that the shift away from Roosevelt, in Iowa, occurred during the drought of 1936, and that in the three years 1937-1940 he was gaining support.

Since the presidential election was held toward the end of the year, after the harvest, it would be ideal to obtain an index of the farmer's cash income by county for 1936. Unfortunately, such data are not available; hence, some indicator of the cash income had to serve. As already observed, the sale of corn and hogs constituted the major part of the farmer's gross income. Since the price was fairly high, the amounts produced per county would give a relative distribution of cash income.[34] Although four-fifths of this income came from the sale of hogs, other factors affected this income and hence the corn production index was selected.[35]

The cash income for 1936 was mostly a function of the drought rather than a function of a long-run factor like average productivity of the soil. Production for 1936 was subtracted from that for 1935 and the difference was used as a net shift in corn production analogous to the net shift in the Roosevelt vote from 1932 to 1936.[36] A paired comparison of these two factors indicated a significant positive relationship between heavy net corn loss and high net vote loss to Roosevelt.[37]

It appears that the distributions of the various long-run factors, measuring the economic status of the different sections of the state, do not substantiate the theory (when compared with the Roosevelt 1936 vote) that Roosevelt attracted all of the most economically depressed portions of the population. The southern counties, which comprise the poorest sections of the state, most staunchly opposed Roosevelt; while the cash grain area, one of the wealthiest parts of the state, gave him the strongest support. Though the entire western meat area is economically well off, its central portion was fairly strong for Roosevelt and its southern portion was very weak.[38] It must be remembered in this connection that the population of the state is relatively homogeneous, without the extremes of poverty and wealth found in such neighboring states as Wisconsin with its northern cut-over areas and Illinois with its southern eroded and flood infested districts.

In Iowa other variables must be sought in explaining party lines or tradition in the long run. While the Roosevelt votes of 1932 and 1936 were little short of revolutionary in view of the Democratic inertia of the preceding decades, a definite relationship is discernible between the voting behavior in the prosperous twenties and the dismal thirties. The similarity of the pattern for 1924 and 1932 confirms the hypothesis that Roosevelt's support came primarily from the combination of the votes of traditional Democrats and former Progressives. In 1924 the Progressive party split the Democratic vote considerably and the Republican vote to a lesser extent. The farm population had experienced a tremendous depression in 1921-1922 following the war boom, and the most discontented elements followed the national pattern of splitting to support La Follette. After 1924, though agriculture continued to decline, the great industrial expansion and general prosperity of the country tended to keep the Republicans in favor and to restore the Democrats to their united strength in 1928.[39] This hypothesis is substantiated in a much more striking fashion by using the actual votes cast for Smith in 1928, Roosevelt in 1932, and Brookhart in the Republican primary of 1932.[40] In other words, after the primary of 1932 anyone who assumed that Roosevelt's vote in the fall election would be the Smith vote plus the Brookhart vote would have almost hit the nail on the head.

In order to determine the relative strength of party tradition through the period 1924-1936, a study was made of the distribution of the average Republican vote for 11 elections.[41] Though the pattern did not coincide neatly with the economic divisions of the state, the southern pasture area, a relatively poor district, had decidedly Republican traditions. The western meat area—prosperous as a whole, though more strongly Democratic than any other section— had a solid Republican southern section. The cash grain area, the best farming district in the state, was quite strongly Republican except for six counties. The dairy area (poor) and the east central meat area (wealthy) were more evenly balanced. In other words, both the wealthiest and the poorest sections had strong Republican fixations, whereas the regions in between were divided more evenly between the major parties. Iowa as a whole is a well-to-do farming state, but such variations in wealth as exist are not closely associated with long-term political alignments.

An examination of the density map for Roosevelt's 1936 vote (Figure 10) shows that there is a much closer correspondence be-

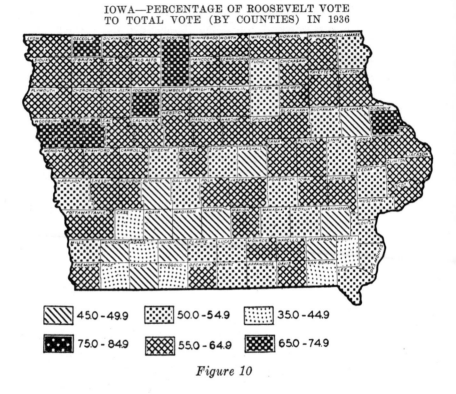

IOWA—PERCENTAGE OF ROOSEVELT VOTE
TO TOTAL VOTE (BY COUNTIES) IN 1936

Figure 10

tween the Roosevelt vote in that year and the average Democratic
vote than with Roosevelt's own vote in 1932. This follows from the
fact that in 1932 the Democrats made their greatest gains in hitherto
strongly Republican areas.

Conclusions from such data are of necessity not very precise.
Iowa, on the average, shifted 4.5 per cent away from Roosevelt in
1936. Many persons still had strong Republican leanings, and,
moreover, the state as a whole suffered from the drought. In the
western meat area both the forces of tradition and of economic ad-
versity were at work. The entire meat area was hit by drought, but

IOWA—PERCENTAGE OF ROOSEVELT VOTE
TO TOTAL VOTE (BY COUNTIES) IN 1940

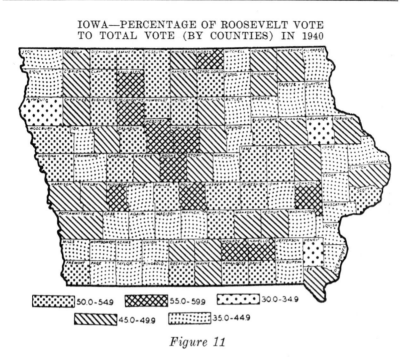

Figure 11

in the traditionally Democratic central counties—Carroll, Crawford, Shelby, and Plymouth—though the shift was strongly anti-Roosevelt, more than 55 per cent of the vote went to the President. On the other hand, in counties like Cass, Page, and Montgomery, as well as in the southern pasture area which they adjoin, the effects of the drought apparently combined with traditional Republicanism to push the Roosevelt support generally below 50 per cent.

A comparison of the maps for 1936 and 1940 elections (Figures 10 and 11) shows the nature of the shift in the major party vote. Roosevelt's average county loss in Iowa was nine per cent, the same as in California.[42] While this average Iowa loss was little more than half of that in Wisconsin, parts of Iowa showed losses as great as in the La Follette stronghold. The 1940 election really revealed a new pattern in Iowa politics. Those regions which had been more strongly Democratic than others during the preceding sixteen years went Republican, and certain sections which were once strongly Republican went Democratic. Party tradition was strongest in the southern part of the state and in those sections of the dairy and eastern meat areas that were nearest the center of the state. In other words, Roosevelt's losses were greatest in the northern part of the western meat area and in the eastern counties bordering on the Mississippi. Western Iowa behaved in a manner similar to that of the adjoining drought states.

As has been said, most of the relatively depressed elements of the southern Iowa farmers did not tend to shift consistently to a support of the Democratic party. This may be due in part to the strong grip of Republicanism, which dates from the Homestead Act of 1862. The Republican party has always played up the pioneering, individualistic and industrious "ideal American farmer." Undoubtedly many farmers, particularly the older ones, were still susceptible to this propaganda despite increasing mortgages, foreclosures, and tenancy. Republican leaders in Iowa, such as Senator L. J. Dickinson, who in 1936 was considered for the Republican Presidential nomination, still ignore economic realities by simultaneously proposing higher tariffs and opposing crop restriction. The efforts of Henry A. Wallace as Secretary of Agriculture and other New Dealers to make the farmers see their economic position more clearly has not gone for naught, but the southern area has not yet been won over.[43] Perhaps the huge government spending worried the farm owners of Iowa. It should be remembered that tenancy is relatively least prevalent in the southern counties and most prevalent in the cash grain area; hence the theme, Balancing the Budget, so strongly played up by the Republicans tended to have more effect among the southern Iowa farmers than in sections where tenancy is more common. Furthermore, these farmers are the most susceptible traditionally to Republican dogma.

In addition to the influence of party tradition, the relation of the prohibition issue to the Roosevelt votes was investigated.[44] About 60 per cent of the electorate approved the repeal amendment submitted in 1933.[45] Those counties which voted heavily for repeal also tended to vote strongly for Roosevelt. The driest parts of the state are the southern pasture area (except urban Lee and Des Moines counties at its eastern end) and the southern part of the western meat area. These sections are practically identical with the traditional Republican strongholds.

There is a strong presumption that other influences, personal or organizational in character, were at work. The Farm Bureau, a pro-New Deal organization, was strongest in the cash grain area and other pro-Roosevelt reas. In the western meat area, the Farmers' Holiday and the Farmers' Union had concentrated membership. On the other hand, a Republican radio station operated by Henry Field, an influential seed man, covered the western part of the southern pasture area and the southern part of the western meat area.[46] Field, in his first attempt at politics, defeated veteran Smith W. Brookhart for senator in the primary of 1932.[47] In 1936, Field supported Landon.

Party organization and discipline was undoubtedly a considerable force in the 1936 presidential election. The *Des Moines Register* went so far as to say on November 2, 1936, that for the first time in many years the Democrats had an effective party organization and that the Republican organization approached its old form. The success of the parties in getting their constituents to vote both the national and state ticket was used an an index of party discipline. The Roosevelt votes of 1932 and 1936 were compared with the senatorial and gubernatorial votes of the same years. The 1932 analysis showed a great amount of ticket splitting.[48] In 1936, however, there was considerably less splitting than in 1932.[49] In both election years Roosevelt ran ahead of the Democratic senatorial and gubernatorial candidates, more so in 1932 than in 1936. It is interesting to note that counties in which Roosevelt ran further ahead in 1936 were in the cash grain area. This would indicate that this area was supporting the national administration, which was responsible for its AAA benefits, more than the state Democratic party. Thus, from 1932 to

1936 the Iowa Democrats took advantage of the patronage placed in their hands by creating a much more efficient organization—one that could successfully associate its local candidates with a powerful national figure.[50]

In 1938 the Democrats lost the governorship and with that the state patronage. The party organization that faced the third term issue in 1940 was, therefore, not as strong as that which carried the state for Roosevelt in 1936. Although Wallace, a native son, ran for vice president, he was not able to save the state for his party. It is probable, however, that his presence on the ticket helped to reduce Willkie's vote. Willkie received only 52 per cent of the total votes in Iowa, whereas in Nebraska he received 57 per cent. Considering Iowa's relationship to the national vote in recent elections, Willkie's margin should have been much greater.[51]

Party discipline in Iowa as measured by the extent to which straight tickets were voted was apparently strong in 1940.[52] There were no factional quarrels which encouraged split ticket voting as in the twenties.

In order to get some idea of the relative importance of the different variables discussed, it is necessary to express the 1936 presidential vote in Iowa as a function of them.[53] Such a study shows that the greatest weight should be given to party tradition as measured by the Roosevelt vote in 1932. It has already been demonstrated that this percentage was a composite of the traditional Democratic and Progressive vote.[54]

A comparison of different relationships is necessary in order to gauge accurately the changes in the areas of Roosevelt support. In the first place, it is important to note that the relationship between the two elections as shown by the Iowa counties is not as close as, for instance, that between the two elections for selected units within the city of Chicago.[55] A study of other relationships shows that, other things being equal, Roosevelt held the wet vote in Iowa in 1936;[56] lost some of the rural farm vote,[57] losing most heavily in those areas which the corn losses were greatest.[58] It is also interesting to note that he lost in those counties where the percentage of native whites was highest.[59]

But other things were not equal. The interrelationships of these variables were such that the net influence of each was concealed.[60] A solution of this problem by means of standard formulae shows that the relationship between the two elections does not change much when allowance is made for other influences; the same can be said of the relationship between the 1936 Roosevelt percentage and the native white percentage. The importance of the net corn loss increases, the relationship with the wet vote is changed from a positive to an inverse one, and the inverse relationship with the rural farm percentage is slightly accentuated.[61]

The relationship of these four influences to the 1936 Roosevelt percentage has already been expressed in functional form.[62] The bulk of the voters did not change their affiliations as between the two elections. However, the analysis shows that, among those who did change, the greatest shifts away from Roosevelt between the two elections were in the counties where the voters were predominantly dry, native white, and farmers who had suffered considerable corn loss. Roosevelt held his ground or gained in 1936 in those counties where there were large percentages of pro-repeal, foreign born, city dwellers, and farmers who suffered only small losses in corn production.

It was also decided to study shifts in the popularity of the New Deal during the thirties. First the difference was obtained between the Roosevelt percentage in 1932 and 1936 by counties, and then these figures were related to other county data.[63] This analysis confirmed the conclusions reached by the other methods described. The pattern of Iowa politics under the New Deal went through minor variations but the main lines remained fairly constant.

Summary

In the short run, those counties suffering most heavily from the drought generally shifted more decidedly against Roosevelt. In the long run, however, many non-economic forces compete with economic factors to bring the latter much out of line with respect to the density distribution of the Roosevelt vote. Thus, the southern counties, which gave Roosevelt the least support, constituted the poorest section of the state and also had the most native white, the "driest" voters, the largest proportion of older people, the most rapidly declining population, the fewest big cities, the smallest number of tenants and farm laborers, and an active Republican radio station. On the other hand, the cash grain area, which gave Roosevelt the greatest support, comprised the wealthiest section of the state and also had the largest population of foreign stock, relatively "wet" voters, the largest proportion of young people, the largest urban area, and the largest number of tenants and farm laborers. Economic deprivation brought an immediate reaction against the Hoover administration, but the nature and extent of the shift was conditioned by the traditional non-economic attitudes toward the major parties.

CHAPTER VI

UTOPIAS IN CALIFORNIA

SOME of the milder epithets which have been applied to California in recent years are "the great and screwy state," and "the crackpot state." In the popular mind, California has long been a state apart from the rest of the nation, where the exotic, the unusual, and the peculiar grow in great profusion—both in nature and in human institutions. Nowhere else has there been such a proliferation of religious sects, of naturopaths, of faith healers, and of spiritualists. The political sphere has not escaped infection. The EPIC (End Poverty in California), Utopian Society, Townsend plan, $30-Every Thursday, and Ham and Eggs movements, bear ample testimony to the willingness of the California electorate to experiment with the politically bizarre. Many hypotheses have been advanced to explain this phenomenon. The climate, the demography, the prevailing agricultural technology have all been suggested as causative factors.[1] However, little has been done thus far to investigate the subject empirically. This chapter is a pioneering attempt, making especial use of voting returns and certain social and economic data.

As noted in Chapter II, California is one of the states that swings with the nation in presidential elections but more violently so. It is typical of a bloc of states in the northwestern United States that has nourished progressive movements and agrarian revolts. Before the depression of the thirties California was rabidly Republican and since 1930 it has been strongly pro-New Deal. Republicans held the governorship from 1898 to 1938. They had a majority in the state assembly from 1898 to 1937 and in the state senate from 1889 to the present. The California political situation strikingly resembles that in Wisconsin. In both cases, the state Democratic party was quite weak (in some counties, almost non-existent), and the voters were divided between progressives and stand-patters—but both groups belonged to the Republican party. Hiram Johnson, leader of the progressive Republicans, was California's counterpart of Wisconsin's La Follette. Like La Follette, Johnson was a veteran campaigner for agrarian liberal causes. He was a Western isolationist, governor of the state from 1911 to 1917, and has been a member of the Senate ever since, voting with the "progressive" bloc.

As in Wisconsin, the depression revived the Democratic party in California. The Democrats garnered great support for Roosevelt in 1932 and a tremendous vote in 1936; at the same time, they were successful in capturing a relatively large number of seats in both the state and national legislatures. Another indication of this tremendous and sudden increase in Democratic strength is furnished by primary election registration statistics. Before 1932, only about 20 per cent of the total registration of voters was Democratic; beginning with 1932, there was a steady increase, and by 1938 about 60 per cent of all registered voters were Democratic.

Along with the sudden resurgence of the Democratic party, came the depression-born Utopian movements—Upton Sinclair's EPIC campaign of 1934, the Utopian Society of 1935, the perennial Townsend plan, and the Ham and Eggs pension plan in 1938 and 1939. Since both Democratic resurgence and Utopian movements appeared after 1930, it would seem *a priori* that some relationship exists between voting attitudes in California and economic conditions. Also, the fact that only California has given birth to so large a number of political panaceas suggests that social conditions in that state perhaps differ materially from those in other states.

Economic Influences on Voting

The 1924 presidential election, the first in the period we are considering, presents a clear-cut issue of liberalism versus conservatism. It was epitomized by the elder La Follette, the Progressive and Socialist candidate, and Calvin Coolidge, the Republican nominee. John W. Davis, the Democratic candidate, was a minor factor in California. If there are differences in the socio-economic composition of the adherents of liberalism and conservatism, they should certainly appear in this election. An analysis of the county returns shows that those who voted for Coolidge came largely from sections which were later anti-New Deal.[2] There was also a very slight tendency for the Coolidge vote to come from the non-agricultural and "dry" parts of the state.[3] La Follette's vote shows a rather definite sectional configuration. A group of fifteen counties gave La Follette 45 per cent or more of their total vote, averaging 49 per cent. Except for San Diego, all of these counties are clustered in the northern part of the state. Mining and lumbering are highly important in twelve of these counties.

The lumberjacks and miners of the Pacific Northwest, which includes northern California, have had a long history of radicalism. The Western Federation of Miners and the I.W.W. were important forces in the lumbering and metal mining industries of this region, for many years, especially before World War I. The tendency, therefore, for the northern California counties to vote comparatively strongly for a progressive candidate may be, in part, due to the radical tradition still strong there. It is noteworthy, also, since in recent years the liberal and radical vote has been heavily concentrated in large cities throughout the country, that almost all the predominantly

Progressive and Socialist California counties are sparsely populated and have few cities of any size. Whether or not this tendency continued through the depression will be discussed below.

Rural-Urban Influences

Writers on California politics have emphasized the decisive role played by the rural-urban factor. Indeed, many California elections have been treated by newspaper commentators as little more than a renewal of the old struggle between city and country. In order to learn something about this factor, an analysis was made of the most rural and most urban counties. It was decided to study northern and southern urban counties separately, since their behavior differed markedly. The seven most urban northern counties, the five most urban southern counties and the ten most rural counties were used for purposes of comparison. The average of the percentages on each issue of the counties making up each sector, was employed as a measure of the behavior of that sector.

The data support the thesis that the rural-urban cleavage, like every other type of social cleavage in California, follows no definite pattern. It re-emphasizes, however, the divergence between the northern and southern sections. In only two of the elections studied did the rural areas run true to form. One was the Upton Sinclair campaign of 1934, in which the anti-Sinclair propaganda, emphasizing the alleged atheistic, Communist attitudes of the Democratic candidate appeared to have had more effect upon the farmer than upon the urbanite. The other was the vote on the anti-picketing initiative bill of 1938, in which the rural areas were the most anti-labor. On the other hand, the vote for Roosevelt in 1932 and 1936, which is often taken as a measure of anti-conservative attitudes, points to another conclusion. Roosevelt received, on the average, a higher vote in the rural counties in 1932 than in either urban section and in 1936 and 1940 a higher rural vote than in the southern urban counties. In most of the recent elections, in fact, the farmers seemed to fit in somewhere between their northern and southern city cousins.

If it had been possible to separate the farm owners from farm laborers, a different state of affairs might have been found. California's agricultural economy differs markedly from that of most states in that a large proportion of the farmers do not own land but are laborers on huge fruit and vegetable farms. In 1936, for example, three-fifths of those engaged in agriculture in California were wage-earners, and 2 per cent of California farms contained one-fourth of all farm acreage.[4] The wage-earners, whether rural or urban, have more in common than does the farm wage-earner with the farm owner. Probably the latter were highly conservative, but their employees tended to vote for radical candidates. This resulted in the confused picture which the sectional analysis reveals.

Despite the absence, then, of statistical data concerning the voting behavior of the two rural groups, there is much evidence of a rural cleavage similar to the laborer-employer cleavage in the city. The large farm owners of California have long been notorious for their reactionary labor policies. For decades they have tapped the sources of cheap labor, first in the Orient, then in Mexico, and during the last decade, in the native white groups of the southwest. Vigilantism, payment of starvation wages, and bloody strike breaking has characterized the activities of large farm owners. They also backed the anti-picketing initiative and fought the single tax and the $30-Every-Thursday measures in 1938. A large number banded themselves into the reactionary organization, Associated Farmers, which seeks to abolish unionism among farm laborers and in feudal fashion retain complete power over large numbers of employees. In the last few years migratory farm workers have been increasingly unionized. As a result, bitter clashes have occurred between striking laborers and the hired guards of the Associated Farmers. What are the implications of this agricultural strife for California politics?

Heretofore, both sides have, for the most part, resorted to economic weapons. Until the thirties, in fact, the laborers had no other choice, since a large proportion were Orientals without the rights of citizenship. But today, the majority of California's 250,000 migratory workers are native Americans. Such a group, if they can establish local residence, will become a potent force in politics. In California, more than in almost any other state, it is possible that the rural-urban issue, long an important factor in American state and national politics, may disappear. Instead there will be a political division along economic lines, with the workers in the city factories and in the "factories in the fields" aligned against their employers.

San Francisco and Los Angeles

Perhaps the outstanding political division in California politics has been the cleavage between northern and southern parts of the state, which goes back to the beginning of statehood. In the 1850's, shortly after California was admitted to the Union, there was considerable agitation for separation into two states; only the Civil War prevented the execution of the plan. Even as recently as 1928 there was much discussion of the possibility of dividing California into two states.[5] The schism is partly geographical, partly historical, and partly demographic. The northern part of the state, starting roughly at the Tehachapi Mountains, is the more staid and settled. It contains a large industrial area centering around San Francisco Bay, many counties whose principal source of livelihood is mining, forestry, or fishing, and several fruit-raising areas. Much of northern California is rugged, mountainous, and sparsely populated; it has experienced a comparatively slow (for California), steady growth in recent years.

In contrast, southern California has a "new" population. Although some of its settlements date back to the sixteenth century, their huge growth occurred in recent decades. This is the best known part of California—Hollywood, orange groves, oil wells, religious sects, and bizarre architecture—the mecca of thousands of retired middle-western farmers and business men, and (in more recent years) more thousands of "Okies," the poverty-stricken, landless farmers of the Southwest.

A comparison of the political activity of the counties containing the "capitals" of the two sections, San Francisco and Los Angeles, may throw some light on the differences between the areas. From these data it would appear that the two counties showed strong contrasts prior to the thirties, but that in recent years these have tended to disappear. In 1924, La Follette received 46 per cent of San Francisco's vote, compared to the 27 per cent given him by Los Angeles. This may be partially attributed to the fact that Los Angeles was notoriously an "open shop" town, where the conservative business and retired middlewestern elements were dominant. San Francisco, on the other hand, had been for years a highly unionized area, and although its labor strength had declined, it still had a much more liberal outlook than its southern neighbor.

During the later 1920's, the prohibition issue seems to have been the dominant dividing factor. The Democratic candidates for governor in 1926 and for president in 1928 ran on pro-repeal platforms. They received 18 and 29 per cent, respectively, of the Los Angeles vote, and 40 and 51 per cent, respectively, of the San Francisco vote. On the other hand, the Democratic candidate for senator in 1926 and governor in 1930 ran on dry platforms, and the tables were completely turned. They received 42 and 36 per cent, respectively, of Los Angeles' vote and 35 and 10 per cent, respectively, from San Francisco. Prohibition was again an outstanding issue in 1932. William G. McAdoo, the Democratic senatorial candidate, had always been a strong upholder of prohibition. In this election he modified his stand somewhat, but was still looked upon as a "dry." Robert P. Shuler, the Prohibition candidate, ran on a bone-dry ticket, and Tallant Tubbs, the Republican aspirant, strongly favored repeal. Tubbs received only 23 per cent of Los Angeles' vote, but 60 per cent of San Francisco's.

Prior to the New Deal, and throughout the early part of the depression, then, the two most important California counties were little concerned with party labels, but much interested in the stand of the candidates on the repeal of the 18th Amendment. Los Angeles, the haven of the retired middlewestern farmer, largely Protestant native white in its composition, was a prohibitionist stronghold and gave a relatively high vote—regardless of party—to the candidates who espoused this cause. San Francisco, the more cosmopolitan area, with almost two-thirds of its population of foreign birth or parentage and about one-fourth Catholic, favored the wet candidates.

Since 1932 the voting behavior of the two counties has been surprisingly similar. The variations in the per cent of their votes going to the Democratic candidates never differed by more than 7 per cent. In the presidential elections of 1932 and 1936 both metropolitan areas were strongly pro-Roosevelt, although San Francisco was somewhat more so than Los Angeles. However, this apparent similarity hides a tremendous difference. In 1932 the northern county had increased its Democratic vote for president only 31 per cent over 1928, but Los Angeles had more than doubled both the absolute number and percentage. How can this sudden about-face on the part of conservative, Republican Los Angeles be explained?

Several reasons suggest themselves. Both counties were suffering greatly from unemployment at this time. This naturally led to great dissatisfaction with the status quo on the part of the lower economic classes, and inspired a protest vote against the Republican administration which had done little to give them relief. Probably, however, a large part of the economically depressed of San Francisco were already Democrats and merely continued to vote the same ticket. On the other hand, Los Angeles, a Republican stronghold in previous elections, had a large reservoir of disgruntled Republicans from whom the resurrected Democratic party could draw its strength.

In addition to this change in the conditions and attitudes of the old residents of the two counties, differentials in the increase in population may have been a factor in the pronounced political shift of Los Angeles. Data are not available for the increase in population between 1928 and 1932, but estimates have been made for the period 1930-1934. These indicate that the Los Angeles' population rose 12.3 per cent and San Francisco's only 4.3 per cent.[6] Probably the same trend occurred between 1928 and 1932. During the depression, much of the migration into California probably consisted of the lower economic strata in search of jobs and a milder climate, rather than retired wealthy persons. If this is true, then Los Angeles' new population swelled the ranks of those dissatisfied with the Republican rule in 1932.

Once the reversal had been accomplished, Los Angeles and San

Francisco followed remarkably similar paths, considering their divergent political behavior in pre-depression days. Although Los Angeles has been called the "metropolis of isms," the record shows that San Francisco is not very far behind. Thus, Los Angeles gave Upton Sinclair 42 per cent of its vote in 1934, and San Francisco 39 per cent, hardly an important difference. Both counties were among the highest in the state for Sinclair. However, the vote for the conservative Governor Frank F. Merriam was much larger in Los Angeles than in San Francisco. Again in 1938 and 1939 when the $30-Every Thursday initiative was on the ballot, 47 per cent of the Los Angeles electorate and 41 per cent of the San Francisco electorate voted in its favor. Most significant of all is the vote on the 1938 measure which would have practically outlawed picketing in California. Los Angeles, a decade earlier one of the leading open shop cities of the country, voted even more strongly against it (61 per cent) than did the highly unionized San Francisco (57 per cent). Most of this change may undoubtedly be attributed to the fact that a strong unionization drive was carried on in Los Angeles in 1937-1938. As a result, the gainfully employed population which was unionized in Los Angeles City rose from 5 per cent (1934) to 34 per cent—just a little less than the San Francisco percentage.[7] The labor issue may, from now on, cease to be a strong basis of dissension between the two metropolitan areas.

After 1932, the trend toward New Dealism in both counties continued at an equal pace. In 1936 both showed an increase in the pro-Roosevelt vote of eight per cent over 1932. In 1938, moreover, both counties for the first time, in the period under discussion, gave majorities to the Democratic and New Deal candidates for governor and senator and thus made possible the election of both. However, whereas San Francisco in 1936 was more Democratic than Los Angeles, the reverse was true in 1938. This is attributable to the fact, noted above, that Los Angeles leads in "isms." Culbert L. Olson and Sheridan Downey, the Democratic candidates in 1938 for governor and senator, respectively, were previously identified with Townsendism and Upton

Sinclair. Hence they made a stronger appeal to the movements' more numerous adherents in the southern metropolis.

In summary, Los Angeles and San Francisco represented in the early part of the period 1924-1940—markedly different views on political and social questions. These views to a great extent reflected differences in the nativity, rate of growth, and character and conditions of employment of their populations. The depression, especially with its concomitants of unemployment and migration, affected both areas but it wrought profound changes in the political attitudes of Los Angeles—transforming a former Republican stronghold into a citadel of the New Deal. In the 1930's, both areas were rather favorably disposed toward the various political aberrations of the depression, and Democratic gains were consolidated and increased until both metropoli were looked upon as certain Democratic territory. However, they represent, in reality, two phases of the growth of the Democratic party. San Francisco has a large bloc of traditional old line Democrats, to which have been added a large number attracted by the New Deal. Los Angeles' Democratic strength is almost entirely a mushroom growth of the thirties. Much of the party support is drawn from ex-radicals, Sinclairite Democrats, and a large number of disgruntled Republicans. Whether such a conglomeration provides a permanent basis of strength for the Democratic party remains to be seen.

Political Factors

The most striking fact that emerges from a study of partisan behavior in California in the period 1924-1940 is the almost complete absence, in many of these years, of any party discipline. One method of measuring discipline is to show the relationship of the per cent vote per county received by a candidate for state office of a given party to the per cent vote per county received by a candidate of the same party for national office. Although national and state officers were elected together five times in California during the period, it was possible to use this measure for only three occasions. Hiram John-son, when running for reelection as senator in 1928, received 75 per cent of the votes. By 1934 his popularity had grown to such an extent that he ran on the Republican, Democratic, and several minor tickets and received 95 per cent of the total vote. These two elections, then, exhibit a lack of discipline since there was, in reality, no important opposition party. Only 1926, 1932, and 1938 can be studied for evidence of party organization.

A comparison of the votes for the Democratic candidates for senator and governor in 1926 shows practically no correlation. In fact, there was a slight tendency for one candidate to get a high vote where the other got a low vote, and vice versa. The opposed views of the two Democrats on the prohibition issue transcended party lines. In 1932, when Senator McAdoo ran for reelection,[8] he not only fell far behind the President, but the variations in his vote did not always closely follow those of Roosevelt. Hence, it may be said that voting discipline in the Democratic party in 1932 was only fair, although much higher than in 1926. Several factors discussed above account for this. McAdoo was a dry who had turned slightly moist for the occasion,[9] and hence he did not gain votes in the same places and in the same amounts as did Roosevelt, an outright wet. In addition, McAdoo was looked upon as more conservative than Roosevelt at a time when high political value was not placed on conservatism. By 1938 a considerable improvement had occurred in the Democratic party discipline. The votes of Olson for governor, and Downey for senator, were highly correlated.[10] In general, these two received the same proportions of their votes in the same areas. Both were at one time identified with Townsendism and Sinclairism, supported Roosevelt, campaigned as "liberals," and strongly opposed the anti-labor initiative. It was their similar stands on important issues, rather than adherence to the same party symbol, which probably resulted in seemingly high party discipline.

The general conclusion may be drawn, even from the sparse data available, that until recently, at any rate, issues and men, not party labels, influenced voting behavior at any one election in California. Whether the high discipline of 1938 presages an increase of party organization with straight ticket voting, cannot be predicted.

Evidence that the trend toward partisan voting is perhaps taking place is furnished by the data on partisan registration. The percentage of those registering who refuse to declare their affiliation with any party fell steadily between 1924 and 1941. Today it constitutes a negligible proportion of the total electorate. If this trend continues, it will be contrary to the trend toward more independent voting appearing almost everywhere else in the country.[11]

Although there is little evidence of coordination between state and national party organizations in California at any election, there was perhaps a tendency for voters to adhere to the same party over a series of years. In studies of other areas—Chicago, Wisconsin, and Pennsylvania, for example—the factor of "party tradition" was found to be of greatest importance in accounting for victories at the polls. There was always a rather large core in each party who voted the party ticket, irrespective of the candidates or issues. The Solid South is, of course, the example *par excellence* of this type of behavior.

One way of measuring the strength of party tradition is to compare the percentages given the candidates for the same office and, if possible, from the same party in successive elections. The data reveal that during the entire period under discussion there was relatively little traditional voting in California except in presidential elections.[12] The 1928 vote for Al Smith, for example, was based to some extent on a combination of the Democratic and Progressive votes of 1924. Roosevelt's vote in 1932, although much higher in every section than Smith's, nevertheless followed a rather similar pattern of variation among the counties.

The highest degree of voting tradition in the whole period was shown in the Democratic votes for 1932, 1936, and 1940. (See Figures 12 and 13.) This is, perhaps, to be expected since the same candidate ran each time. On the whole, voters in California changed their party allegiance from election to election in accordance with changing issues and personalities rather than adhered to any party symbol.

If on the national political stage California presents a confused

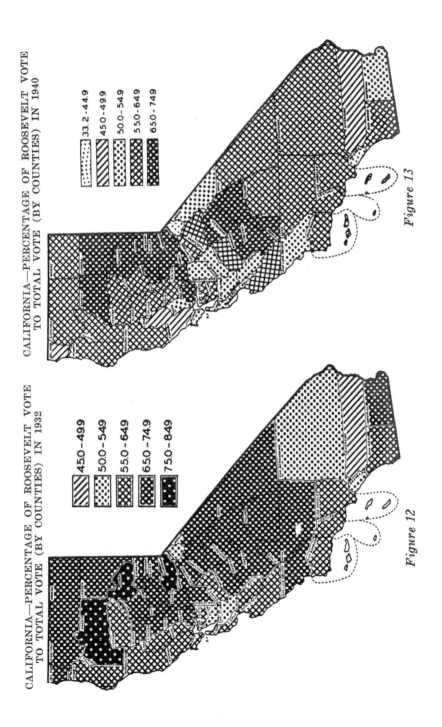

CALIFORNIA—PERCENTAGE OF ROOSEVELT VOTE
TO TOTAL VOTE (BY COUNTIES) IN 1940

33.2 - 44.9
45.0 - 49.9
50.0 - 54.9
55.0 - 64.9
65.0 - 74.9

Figure 13

CALIFORNIA—PERCENTAGE OF ROOSEVELT VOTE
TO TOTAL VOTE (BY COUNTIES) IN 1932

45.0 - 49.9
50.0 - 54.9
55.0 - 64.9
65.0 - 74.9
75.0 - 84.9

Figure 12

picture so far as party tradition and discipline are concerned, the state scene is almost chaotic. Because of a liberal primary law, a person can file as a candidate in as many party primaries as he chooses. However, a candidate who does not win the nomination of his own party cannot have the nomination of any other party, no matter how large a majority he rolls up.[13] Coupled with these provisions are others providing that anyone can change his party affiliation before the primary merely by declaring his intention to do so.[14] As the result of these laws, party designations have been largely meaningless in California state legislative politics. Many candidates receive the Republican and Democratic nominations, and encounter opposition only from some minor party candidate.

An examination of the composition of the California legislature during the period 1925-1940 reveals the extremely minute role of the Democratic party in state politics until recently, and the important part played throughout this period by men running as nominees of both major parties. One observer attributes this situation partly to the fact that the California electorate, like that of several other western states, habitually used the Republican party as the instrument of reforms.[15] However, in the Republican primaries of 1930, the reform branch of the party was badly defeated when the Progressive-Republican group under Hiram Johnson revolted and joined the Democratic minority.

Since the depression the Democrats have continued to grow until they outnumber the Republicans (as distinguished from the Republican-Democrats) in the legislature. This trend appears to have been accompanied, to a slight extent, by a reduction in the number of political bi-partisans in the legislature.

Although, as has been shown above, personal and factional politics were the rule in California, certain counties quite consistently voted Democratic or strongly Republican. In these counties a traditional vote of a sort can be said to have existed; this was especially true after the advent of the New Deal in 1933. The county analysis discloses some of the roots of the New Deal and anti-New Deal traditional vote. Both in 1928 and 1932, the New Deal counties were already rather strongly Democratic, and hence the Roosevelt vote was based partly on the core of Democratic voters which appeared during presidential election years. Probing a little further into political antecedents of these counties, it was found that not only a pro-Democratic but a Progressive tradition—as evidenced in the vote for La Follette in 1924—contributed to the New Deal electorate in California.

So far as social composition is concerned, there was little discernible difference between the pro- and anti-New Deal areas. Both were predominantly wet, urban and native white. However, in their attitudes toward social questions, distinct cleavages were evident. The Ham and Eggs pension plan was more popular in the New Deal areas than in the strongly Republican districts. On the other hand, the strongly anti-union, anti-picketing initiative of 1938 would have been passed had the decision been left to the traditionally Republican counties, while only a minority (39 per cent) of the population of the New Deal counties favored it. The vote in 1934, when Upton Sinclair was the Democratic gubernatorial candidate, might also be considered an index of attitudes on social questions. This provided an excellent test of whether the traditional New Deal Democratic counties were sufficiently Democratic to support the party when its name was used by a life-long Socialist with somewhat radical doctrines. The results indicate that the party symbol played no significant part as between the two groups of counties. The average vote for Sinclair in each group was about the same (about 32 per cent). However, this does not mean that the two groups reacted in the same way. The anti-New Deal counties strongly favored the conservative Republican, Merriam, giving him almost twice the vote they gave Sinclair, and paying almost no attention to Raymond L. Haight, the third major participant in this tripartite campaign. On the other hand, the New Deal counties, unwilling to support Sinclair (their party's nominee), found Merriam almost as distasteful, and hence voted comparatively strongly for Haight, the middle-of-the-road Republican of liberal sentiments running on an independent ticket.

California as a Whole

How did the influences at work in California combine to produce
the striking voting behavior of recent elections? The answer may
be sought in analyzing either the 1936 or 1940 presidential election.
The most important factor in explaining the result was the traditional Democratic and Progressive vote. This combination first
clearly appeared in the 1928 presidential election. Building on this
foundation, Roosevelt attracted other groups—pro-Labor, wet, and
those in favor of liberal Federal spending—in about equal proportions. The foreign groups (by birth or parentage) were more pro-
Roosevelt than the native groups, but the rural and urban elements
were almost evenly divided. The native farmers who favored prohibition hesitated to support Roosevelt, but farmers who were engaged in raising grapes, those of foreign extraction, and the farm
laborers with uncertain employment were pro-New Deal. California was still loyal to its old Progressive leader, Hiram Johnson, but
it was also partial to the New Deal with its AAA, Social Security,
WPA, PWA, and Defense programs.

CHAPTER VII

RURAL-URBAN CONFLICT: ILLINOIS

ILLINOIS seems to resemble Pennsylvania in its political behavior, but a close examination reveals important differences. While both states are typical of the industrial north (east of the Mississippi) Illinois is dominated by a single huge metropolitan community, in contrast to Pennsylvania, which has several metropolitan centers. Furthermore, Illinois is still a prairie state since, except for the metropolitan region of Chicago and the fifteen southern counties where the extraction of coal and oil are important, it is part of the great farm belt. The politics of the corn, wheat, and dairy sections of Illinois is like that of the neighboring states of Iowa and Wisconsin.

While the other states studied all have large cities, in none does a single metropolitan community take the important place which

Chicago holds in Illinois. Since 1928 one-half the Illinois vote has come from Cook County. However, inasmuch as there has been no reapportionment of the state congressional, legislative, and judicial districts since 1901, the downstate region contains nearly two-thirds of the congressional and state senatorial districts and six-sevenths of the judicial districts.[1] The antagonism between Chicago and "downstate" is a key to many Illinois elections. It is not clearly a rural-urban conflict, since only one-fifth of the downstaters are farmers, but it is a battle between a metropolis which has been growing rapidly until recently and a region which contains a declining rural population and a small city population with a slower rate of increase than Chicago.[2] Albert Lepawsky wrote: "Deliberations at Springfield, the state capital, frequently run counter to the interests of metropolitan Chicago and other Illinois cities because of (1) the legislature's failure to comprehend urban problems, (2) sectional rivalries between Chicago or its sister-cities and the 'downstate' not always based upon actual differences in sectional needs, and (3) political bargainings for patronage and special concessions engaged in by Chicago's representatives as well as by legislators from the remainder of the state."[3]

The antagonism between the metropolis and the rest of the state is in part based upon a struggle for power. The downstaters now hold political power, particularly in the state legislature, and they intend to make every effort to keep the status quo. When a proposal was made recently to reapportion the senatorial districts, one of the downstate senators said, "Who will volunteer to lay his head upon the block?"[4]

The social and economic composition of the two sections of the state has deepened the gulf between them. Only 34 per cent of the inhabitants of the metropolis as compared with 70 per cent of the downstaters are native whites of native parentage. There are twice as many Catholics in proportion to total population in Cook County as in the rest of the state. The Protestant farmers and small townspeople distrust the big city with its Irish, Polish, Jewish, and Italian politicians. On questions relating to the public regulation of morals the conflicting points of view are clearly marked. Whereas in 1930 about half of the downstaters voted dry, about four-fifths of the Chicago region voted wet.[5] Questions relating to taxation and the regulation of business have also divided the two parts of the state.

It has already been pointed out that during the period from 1896 to 1940 Illinois closely paralleled national political trends when allowance was made for its Republican leanings.[6] The Republican bias in Illinois was not as strong as in Pennsylvania, since there always existed a powerful Democratic organization in Chicago and a strong Democratic tradition in the southern part of the state.

During the twenties and thirties the Chicago region showed a tendency to swing more'violently than the rest of the state. In 1924 Cook County was more Republican than the remaining counties but in 1936, 1938, and 1940 it was far more Democratic than downstate.[7] Without its metropolis, Illinois tended to resemble Iowa in its political make-up. The maximum New Deal vote downstate came in 1932 and after that the popularity of Roosevelt and his measures declined.

The more pronounced swings in Cook County were not the result of progressive tendencies, as in Wisconsin. It is true that the labor elements in Chicago showed progressive leanings from time to time, but they did not dominate the political situation. The chief characteristic of the political life of the metropolis was party machine control.[8] During the twenties, both the major parties had strong political organizations in Cook County. The Republic machines were founded on federal and state patronage and a liberal share of the county, city, and special district spoils. One of the Republican factional machines was dominated by the picturesque mayor of Chicago, William Hale (Big Bill) Thompson. His chief opponent was the late United States Senator, Charles S. Deneen, who controlled many federal and county appointments. On the Democratic side, the machine was based upon a portion of the county, city, and special district patronage.

The 1930 elections marked the beginning of an era of Democratic machine domination in Chicago and Cook County. Within a few years the Republicans were completely eliminated from the key posts and the famous Kelly-Nash machine began to function in a smooth running fashion.[9] Within its own bailiwick, this Democratic organization has had few setbacks.[10] It has enjoyed more complete control over governmental patronage within the metropolitan region than any other machine in the history of Chicago. When the downstate section began to slip back into the Republican fold in 1934 and 1936, the Democratic lead in Chicago was increased. In 1938 the Democratic advantage in Cook County was reduced slightly, but the 10 per cent margin between the largest county and the rest of the state was maintained. If it had not been for Cook County the state would have gone Republican in 1938. Roosevelt's lead in Chicago was sufficient to enable him to carry the state in 1940, but the other Democratic candidates did not fare so well (excepting the candidate for secretary of state).

A very good index to the strength of a party organization is the size of its primary vote. Since a voter who participates in an Illinois primary must ask for a ballot of a particular party, much more persuasion is needed to bring out a large vote in a primary than in a general election. The peak of the Illinois Republican primary vote in the past two decades was reached in 1928, when there was a very spirited contest between the leading Republican factions. In Chicago this was called the "pineapple" primary because of the bombing of the homes of John A. Swanson, candidate for state's attorney, and Charles S. Deneen, United States Senator. From 1928 to 1938 there was a steady decline in the size of the Republican primary vote, both in Cook County and downstate, and a corresponding rise in the size of the Democratic primary vote.[11] However, the swing was much more marked in Cook County than in the rest of the state. Whereas in 1928 there were in Cook County nearly 700,000 more Republican than Democratic primary voters, in 1938 the situation was reversed and there were 700,000 more Democratic than Republican primary voters. Except in times of great crisis, a large primary vote is the result of organization efforts. The Democrats in Chicago had the efficient primary vote-getting machinery, made up of office holders, pay rollers, favored contractors, privileged under-

world leaders, beneficiaries of federal and state relief, trade union-
ists, and others.

The trend toward greater participation in the Democratic than
in the Republican primary stopped in 1940. Downstate, the Republican gains among the primary voters were partly related to
Republican 1938 electoral successes, which extended to many county
and local offices; in Chicago, however, Republican gains were associated with a revival of Republican hopes.

During the period 1924-1940 Cook County Democrats and downstate Republicans, with one or two exceptions, comprised a majority
of their respective party primaries. This did not mean that factional lines were always so drawn as to develop intra-party conflict
between Cook County and downstate.[12] Until 1936 the selection of
state candidates by the Cook County Democratic organization was
not effectively challenged. The downstate Democratic primary
voters were not as well marshalled as were the Chicago Democrats
under George Brennan and later under Anton J. Cermak. In the
Republican primaries there were no clear cut battles on the question
of Chicago or downstate domination. Each Cook County Republican
faction had downstate allies, and the rural-urban issue was not
raised. In 1924 the vote for the two leading Republican contenders
for the United States senatorship was so close that the slight advantage of the one in Cook County tipped the scales in his favor.

In 1936 the Cook County control of the Democratic state primaries was shattered.[13] Although Governor Henry Horner was originally a Chicago City Hall candidate, the death of Mayor Cermak
weakened Horner's connections with the Chicago machine leaders.
The new mayor of Chicago, Edward J. Kelly, and his associates, particularly Patrick Nash, chairman of the Cook County Democratic
organization, were cool toward Horner because of his antagonism to
some of their pet legislative schemes. Horner broke openly with the
Kelly-Nash machine when the mayor announced that he was going
to support Herman N. Bundesen, city Health Commissioner, for the
governorship. Horner had been asked to retire gracefully, and was
even offered a federal judgeship as an inducement. Rather than go

on the bench, however, he preferred to take the risk of bucking the machine.

Although the odds against him seemed great at first, his campaign soon gained momentum. The rivalry between Chicago and downstate was aroused by the demands of the city leaders for liberalized gambling laws, for the defeat of bills creating a sound system of registration of voters, and for increased control of state affairs. Governor Horner had vetoed the gambling bills and the defeat of the registration laws in the state Senate played into his hands. Mayor Kelly had protested at the possible loss of 200,000 votes in the coming presidential election because of disfranchisement of persons by the proposed legislation, and this was turned neatly against him. As Horner put it, "Do any of you think President Roosevelt would care to be elected in Illinois by crooked votes? . . . They are still trying to vote butterflies, fence rails, and ghosts, but it is not going to work this year. The people of Illinois are aroused against bossism and they are going to see that 'Boss' Kelly won't rule Illinois."[14]

In building up a rival organization, Governor Horner did not hesitate to use state patronage freely. The Kelly-Nash group tried to discredit his campaign by sensational charges of payroll padding, and the state treasurer even held up some of the payrolls. However, this line of attack fell flat, as it was a case of the kettle calling the pot black. The governor lost the city of Chicago by 150,000 votes, but his margin of 300,000 votes downstate gave him a comfortable lead.

In 1938 Governor Horner's faction repeated this performance when the control of the senatorial nomination was at stake. The Governor backed Scott Lucas, a downstate man, while the Chicago leaders put up Michael Igoe, a Chicagoan who had many downstate connections because of his long service in the state legislature. The anti-Chicago faction won again.

On the basis of previous studies of Chicago politics by the author it is possible to make a number of comparisons between the politics of the metropolis and the rest of the state. The election returns and social data available for the 101 downstate counties may be contrasted with the corresponding data for 144 selected districts in the city of Chicago.[15]

Economic Influences

Are economic deprivations and indulgences more important in the metropolis than downstate in determining political behavior? Do the Chicagoans consider their economic interests more realistically than the farmers, the coal miners, the workers in the oil regions, and the small city dwellers and townsmen? (See Figures 14 and 15.)

One measure of the farm vote is the ratio of the total population that is classified as rural-farm in the United States Census. It has already been indicated that by 1936 the rural-farm elements in Wisconsin and Pennsylvania were in general inclined to swing back to the Republican party in presidential elections. In Iowa this tendency was most marked among the stock raisers who were hit by the drought and the artificially high price of grain; and in Wisconsin and Pennsylvania, the dairy farmers who were not included in the farm programs of the Roosevelt administrations were inclined to oppose the Democrats.

The rural-farm elements of Illinois, taken as a whole, showed no distinct political tendency during the period 1924-1940.[16] However, a sectional analysis reveals that influences similar to those in the other states studied were operating in Illinois. In the dairy areas of the northern part of the state the farmers were anti-New Deal, as in Wisconsin and Pennsylvania.[17] In the livestock regions of northwestern Illinois, the rural-farm elements behaved like those in Iowa. They followed the general revolt against the Republican party in 1932, but by 1936 they were drifting back to the party. The cash grain area of central and eastern Illinois, a Republican stronghold of the twenties, remained Democratic in 1936, as did the farmers in similar areas in Iowa; but by 1938 this area, too, had shifted back to the G.O.P. The price of corn was much lower in 1940 than in 1936, and Roosevelt's losses in the Illinois corn belt were relatively higher in 1940 than in any other sections.

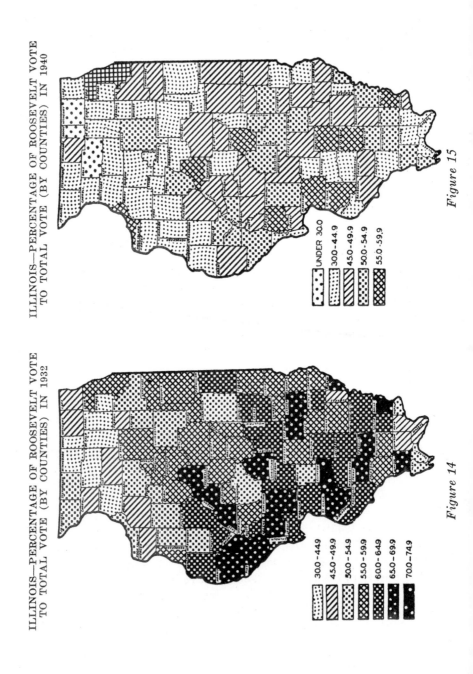

ILLINOIS—PERCENTAGE OF ROOSEVELT VOTE
TO TOTAL VOTE (BY COUNTIES) IN 1940

UNDER 30.0
30.0–44.9
45.0–49.9
50.0–54.9
55.0–59.9

Figure 15

ILLINOIS—PERCENTAGE OF ROOSEVELT VOTE
TO TOTAL VOTE (BY COUNTIES) IN 1932

30.0–44.9
45.0–49.9
50.0–54.9
55.0–59.9
60.0–64.9
65.0–69.9
70.0–74.9

Figure 14

Fortune magazine in 1940 made a special study of a typical Illinois county in the cash grain region and reported:

These businessmen-farmers are almost all conservative Republicans. The small farmers and tenants are traditionally Republican, but hard times have switched their traditions in some elections, notably in 1932 and 1936, and nobody wants to predict for sure what they'll do in 1940. Last year the AAA had more signers in the county than ever before, and they received $365,500 in parity and conservation payments. Corn was nine cents a bushel in 1933, went to ninety-nine cents in 1935, and is now fifty cents. Hogs were four cents a pound in 1933, up as high as twenty-two cents in 1935, and have slipped back to five cents. The Democratic leaders say the farmers won't take a chance on what the Republicans might or might not do. The Republicans say the farmers are getting disgusted with these stopgap subsidies and don't like Secretary Hull's trade agreements. . . . But in DeWitt County, as in many sections of the U. S., even the farmers who grumble loudest about the government are glad to get the checks. ''We'll have to pay for it so we might as well take all we can get.''[18]

The other farming areas in the southern half of Illinois were generally Democratic in the 1930's. In contrast to Chicago, the popularity of the Democratic party declined steadily after 1932 but even in 1938 the southern regions were Democratic by a small margin. These areas, with general farming, wheat and dairy farming, and some poultry raising, have been less specialized than those in the northern part of the state.[19] Many of the southern counties were Democratic in the prosperous twenties not so much because of the party's farm policies as for historical reasons. Southern Illinois is at the same longitude as Kentucky and Missouri, where Democratic traditions have been strong because of migrations from southern states. A notable exception, however, is found in three of the most southerly counties—Johnson, Pope, and Massac—situated in a fruit and vegetable region with very poor soil. This region, racked by soil erosion, floods, and difficult farming conditions, has been traditionally Republican.[20] Its isolated, Protestant native white and colored farmers were less affected by the economic changes of the twenties and thirties than the farmers in other parts of Illinois. In this they resemble certain backward farming communities in Iowa and Pennsylvania. In 1938 the Democratic party undoubtedly was able to retain this section because of the strength of the relief vote.

The political behavior of the more urbanized downstate counties may be explained on a number of grounds. The counties which adjoin Cook County are part of metropolitan Chicago and therefore fit into the urban pattern. The outlying high rental areas of Chicago were traditionally Republican and were the least influenced by the Democratic machine. Commuters and suburbanites in the neighboring counties could be placed in this same classification.[21] Throughout the entire period, they remained Republican, influenced no doubt by the strong Chicago Republican newspapers.

The two Illinois counties in the metropolitan area of St. Louis behaved differently from those near Chicago, in part because they were industrial rather than residential and in part because of the influence of southern migration. As in Chicago as a whole, the popularity of the Democratic party in the counties near St. Louis increased steadily from 1928 until the 1938 congressional elections. In other words, New Deal popularity did not fall off here in 1936 and the region remained Democratic in 1938 and 1940.

The remaining Illinois cities of 50,000 or more population were strongly Republican during the twenties,[22] but Democratic support rose steadily in these cities until 1938. In this respect the downstate cities resembled Chicago and the urban centers of Wisconsin and Pennsylvania. Roosevelt's popularity was greatest in the larger cities, and did not decline in 1936, as it did in the small towns and farm areas.

In southern Illinois there are a half dozen counties in which coal mining is the leading occupation.[23] During the period 1928-1940 they fluctuated very little as compared with other sections of the state. In 1928 the coal-mining counties supported Al Smith for president and the Democratic candidates for congressmen-at-large, and twelve years later they were still in the Democratic column, although some neighboring counties had shifted to the Republicans. The stability of these counties is undoubtedly due to the strength of the labor unions. The United Mine Workers had always been strong in this region, and after joining the C. I. O., they increased in numbers. Under the liberal labor policies of the New Deal, the miners' political power in the area was strengthened. In addition, the depression in the coal industry made the relief load high in these counties, a situation which favored the Democrats. The political behavior of the Illinois coal counties is quite similar to that of the Pennsylvania coal counties.

The oil boom in southern Illinois during the thirties had political repercussions.[24] The Democrats polled their maximum vote in the oil region in 1932; the section was still Democratic in 1938 and 1940, and the decline in Democratic strength in those years was relatively slight. It has been estimated that at least 5,000 Oklahomans with Democratic leanings migrated to this area during the thirties. The relief burden in the oil counties was not as heavy as in the coal counties, but it exerted some influence in maintaining the popularity of the New Deal.

Taking downstate Illinois as a whole, it is clear that economic considerations were not as important as in Chicago. There was comparatively little relationship between economic status and party division until the election of 1938.[25] In that year the relief vote was definitely Democratic. The most prosperous downstate counties showed no marked tendency to vote Republican, except in the immediate neighborhood of Chicago.

Social Influences

Sufficient evidence has been adduced in the preceding chapters to show that too much importance should not be attached to purely economic considerations in trying to explain voting behavior. As in other states, the voters in Illinois were swayed by a complex combination of considerations. Data are available for the analysis of only a few of these.

On no question was antagonism between metropolitan Chicago and downstate more clearly marked than on the liquor question. A number of measures came before the voters, and in each case downstate was twice as dry as Cook County. It appears that the dry sentiment in downstate Illinois did not follow party lines, as it did in Chicago.[26] The Democratic organization in the state, led by the Chicago machine leaders, was dripping wet during the period under discussion, but many dry Democratic counties were found in southern Illinois which voted for Al Smith in 1928 and for Roosevelt in 1932. Some wet counties near Chicago, on the other hand, were strongly Republican. Here the influence of the Republican Chicago *Tribune,* which was then rabidly wet, was manifest.

In Chicago the native whites of native parentage tended to vote Republican, while those of foreign extraction supported the Democrats. Downstate counties showed some slight tendency to group themselves in the opposite fashion.[27]   The counties with the highest ratio of persons of foreign extraction were near Chicago and these, as we have seen, were Republicans. By contrast, the southern counties with the highest ratio of native whites of native parentage were Democratic, many of them traditionally so.[28]

In all the states and communities studied so far, it appears that the closest correlation between Catholicism and the Democratic presidential vote was found in 1928. A tendency persisted in the North for the Catholic voters to support Democratic candidates and for Protestant voters to support Republicans, but it was never again as strong as when a major party nominated a Catholic for president. In downstate Illinois this relationship is slight as compared with Chicago or Pennsylvania.[29]   The strongest Catholic Illinois county, Clinton, was consistently Democratic until 1940, when the popularity of President Roosevelt took a sudden dip. In the northern part of the state the most highly Protestant counties were Republican, but in the southern part there was a powerful Democratic tradition among many Protestants.[30]

Party Tradition, Organization, and Discipline

As has already been made clear, many of the political variations in Illinois counties can be explained chiefly in terms of tradition. Certain regions behaved in a particular fashion over a long period. Here the voters may have been influenced by early family conditioning, or by later environmental circumstances that remained constant. A county by county analysis does not show the process but it indicates the results.

Because two of its congressmen are elected at large, it is possible to study political trends in Illinois more advantageously than in the other states analyzed. The figures available[31] for each county in every even-numbered year are not as subject to the personality differences among candidates as are the presidential figures. Hence, the aggregate congressional returns for the two sets of candidates give a more impersonal view of party strength than the votes for president, governor, or United States senator.

In the twenties and thirties, Chicago was consistently more Democratic than the rest of the state. The peak of Democratic strength downstate was reached in 1932 but in Chicago it was not attained until 1934. By 1938 the Democratic strength had slipped back to the 1930 level downstate, but in Chicago it slipped only to the 1932 level. The 1934 and 1936 elections represented the peaks for the state. In the period 1926-1936 the Democrats in Chicago had gained in the average district 20 per cent of the total vote, whereas in the average downstate county they gained only 13 per cent.

The Democratic gains in Chicago, as compared with those downstate, were not only greater, but more evenly distributed. In other words, the Democratic candidates tended to gain about the same percentage in all parts of Chicago, whereas downstate they gained much more in some counties than in others, and when the party fortunes began to decline they lost in varying amounts.[32] This situation may be said to reflect the growing power of the Democratic city machine, which exerted pressure in all parts of the city. Downstate the Democratic organization was not so efficient in every county.

However, a comparison between downstate Illinois and some of the other states analyzed shows that for a state machine the Illinois Democratic organization was quite powerful. The 13 to 15 per cent average increase in the Democratic vote did not disturb greatly the geographical variations of the Democratic constituency. Those counties which were more strongly Republican or Democratic than the average county in the twenties tended to remain so in the thirties.[33]

The 1940 election returns throw light on the relative strength of party tradition and organization. Especially revealing is an analysis of shifts by counties from 1936 to 1940. As in 1938, the Democratic party continued to decline in the state. However, the loss of votes by the Democratic congressmen-at-large was greater in Chicago than downstate. This is strong proof that a party machine has great difficulty in stopping an electoral swing that is well under way. The Kelly-Nash machine did not lose patronage in the 1938 county elections, but it could not prevent the 1940 Republican gains. However, if the City Hall machine had lost Cook County in 1938, the decline would undoubtedly have been greater. Downstate, those counties which remained Democratic shifted, on the average, two per cent less in 1940 than those which were captured by the Republicans. This means that the Democratic job holders were able to stem the tide against Roosevelt slightly. In counties where the vote of the two parties was very close, the party machine may have been the deciding factor.

The relationship between the votes for different candidates of the same party at the same election has been used to measure party discipline. According to this device, the discipline of the two major parties in Illinois has been very high despite bitter factional quarrels in the primaries. Only in 1932 was there a noticeable difference between Chicago and downstate in the matter of party discipline. In that year there was a pronounced tendency for the anti-Small-Thompson machine in Chicago to cut Len Small, Republican nominee for governor, and support the Democratic candidate, Henry Horner. Horner ran far ahead of Roosevelt in Chicago but downstate there was not so much "knifing" of Small.[34] In 1936 and 1940 party discipline downstate was only slightly less rigorous than in Pennsylvania, which had the most perfect record of any state analyzed. The straight-ticket device used in Illinois, plus the general emphasis upon machine methods, has reduced independent voting to a rather low level.[35]

General View of Illinois Politics

The voting behavior of any Illinois county during the twenties and thirties may be explained largely in terms of party tradition, party organization, economic trends, religious preferences, national origins, and dominant opinions regarding the regulation of public morals. Though the importance of these influences varied from county to county, it is possible to get a general view of the average county.

Taking the elections from 1924 to 1940 as a whole, it is probable that roughly four-fifths of the county variations may be explained in terms of party tradition as measured by previous voting behavior, one-quarter on the basis of national origins, one-quarter on the basis of the variations in the relief load, and the remainder on the basis of moral and religious views and unique considerations.[36] These influences are of course interrelated and the net relationships are not given above. Thus, party tradition is associated with national origins and the other influences, and the religious and moral views are interrelated.[37]

The increase in economic insecurity after 1929 brought a more pronounced reaction against the party in power in Chicago than it did downstate. In the metropolis, the greatest shifts occurred in the outlying lower-middle-class areas, where there were many foreclosures or threatened foreclosures; and the smallest shifts were found in high-class hotel areas and in the sections having many Protestant home-owners who weathered the depression with comparatively little discernible difficulty. Downstate, the greatest shifts were found in the problem areas where the relief burden was heavy, in the oil territory, and in the central Illinois cash grain and general farming areas.

Perhaps one of the most remarkable aspects of Illinois politics in the thirties has been the even spread of the revolt against the Republican party. Only half a dozen counties failed to react against the dominant party of the twenties. This uniformity is in part the product of the powerful political machines that have characterized Chicago and downstate Illinois politics.

CHAPTER VIII

LONG'S LOUISIANA

LOUISIANA is a much discussed but relatively little known state. Its lurid politics and picturesque traditions have in recent years provided a happy-hunting-ground for journalists. However, no scientific treatment has been made of the peculiar yet significant problems of the 2,000,000 people of diverse races, origins, and culture who inhabit the bayous, the hills, and the cotton fields of the state. Although a good many writers have drawn grotesque caricatures of the Louisiana political scene and have pointed with contempt at Huey P. Long's dictatorial state, none have illuminated the workings of his machine sufficiently to indicate how the rise of a Long in other areas might be prevented.

The limitations of the quantitative method of studying political behavior are nowhere so evident as in the study of Louisiana and its leader. Even in a two-party state the behavior of the voters in primary elections does not follow as regular a pattern as in the final elections. In Louisiana where the final election is a foregone conclusion, exclusive reliance must be placed upon the primaries. The lack of a two-party tradition means that the election process itself is not adequately safeguarded. In the northern states reliance is placed upon bi-partisan boards for the conduct of elections. While this system is far from perfect, it is much better than the Louisiana system, where the control of the election machinery is vested in interested persons who may or may not be properly watched. Various election investigations show that the secrecy of the ballot, the honesty of the count, and the integrity of the entire election have been frequently violated in Louisiana.[1] Under these circumstances it is extremely difficult to test rational hypotheses of voting behavior. The election returns may reflect the cleverness of the vote manipulators, not the viewpoints of the voters.

Before the operation of the Long machine from 1925 to 1941 can be understood, something must be known of the background of Louisiana politics and the history and composition of Louisiana society.

Louisiana is not a typical southern state. Its sixty-four parishes have an unusual diversity of racial, religious, and occupational groups. The state was 37 per cent urban in 1920 and 42 per cent urban in 1940. Negroes, who accounted for 36.9 per cent of the population in 1930, are concentrated chiefly along the northeastern Mississippi river basin, and in the northwestern corner of the state. They have not voted in large numbers since 1896 when 130,334 were registered.[2] In 1900 this number dropped to 5,320[3] and in October, 1938 to 1,123.[4] Most of this Negro vote was in New Orleans. In 1928, 42 parishes had no Negro registrants. At the peak of Long's power, an applicant for suffrage, in addition to paying a poll tax and fulfilling certain other requirements, was legally required to demonstrate his ability to read and write unless he had "character" and "understanding," that is, was well disposed to the good order and happiness of the United States and the state, and understood the duties and obligations of citizenship under a republican form of government, and was

able to give a reasonable interpretation of the United States Constitution.[5] In 1934 a constitutional amendment was passed which abolished the poll tax. This was not, however, followed by an increased
registration, since the local machines would pay the tax for a poor
man before repeal. To bar Negroes from the Democratic primaries,
the Democratic party forbade any Negro membership. But events
showed that with or without the vote, the Negro was feared politically
by southern demagogues and insecurity-ridden whites.

The number of foreign-born in Louisiana is small—only 1.7 per
cent of the population. Nevertheless, the effect of a division into
native and foreign-born is simulated by the difference between population of the northern parishes, British in origin, and that of southern
parishes, in large part of French origin. These two large groups
have not yet wholly merged. Aggressive symbols directed against one
group by a politician find receptive ears in the other. The Ku Klux
Klan, for example, found large numbers of followers in the northern
hills of Louisiana. Baptist Protestantism is a far cry from Catholicism
and there are many sources of friction between them. Consequently,
in Louisiana local politics the voters tend to demand identity of re-
ligion between themselves and their representative, though in national
politics they most frequently demand a submergence of the irrecon-
cilable religious issue in order to achieve other common goals desired
by both the northern and southern parts of the state.

Of the church members 13 years of age and over, 56 per cent
are Roman Catholics.[6] The Protestants are thus almost as numerous
as the Catholics but they are split into some thirty or more denomina-
tions, with the Baptists and Methodists outnumbering the others.
The Jewish congregations make up less than 2 per cent of the church
membership. The Catholics are concentrated in some twenty-eight
parishes with the Protestants holding the balance. While anti-
clericalism has not been an issue, the differences between the two main
religious groups sometimes furnishes the basis for political divisions.

It is well then, to keep clearly in mind the two social problems in
Louisiana—the race problem and the religious problem. Their im-

portance in any study of "rational" political behavior cannot be overemphasized.

For a southern state, Louisiana has an unusual amount of economic resources and a wide variety of occupations, founded on distinct geographical divisions. The southern French region is characterized by marshes and lowlands, with trapping, fishing and farming. In the hilly northern part of the state where the soil is poorer, are some of the richest oil fields in the world. Throughout the central and eastern part, cotton farming occupies a prominent place, while scattered over the state are urban centers with their industrial, refining, and commercial outlets. New Orleans, of course, is a cosmopolitan city of nearly half a million and a seaport of the first rank. Its vote is represented in three parishes, Orleans, Jefferson, and St. Bernard.

The cotton farming region of Louisiana is typical of a large part of the deep South. The tenant farmer lives in a hell of poverty and hopelessness; the waste of forests and inefficient use of land are obstacles to cultural and economic advancement. The Louisiana rural population there has a lack of purpose, and a bewilderment in the face of man-made and natural forces which account for many of the peculiar traits of Louisiana politics.[7] Housing conditions in large sections of the state are terribly inadequate; prices, and therefore incomes, are unstable; and there is too little capital for efficient farm management.[8] Economic nationalism had destroyed the cotton farmer's income. In the labor market Negroes offer great competition to the whites. There was no security in Long's Louisiana because the present was dismal and the future more so.

Evidences of social disorganization in the general Louisiana scene made it necessary to seek more exact indices of a disorganized public. The "rational" reaction would be to use political devices, which are specifically designed for that purpose, to correct economic and social defects. But many previous studies have pointed out that politics need not be "rational," that political campaigns may be fought over completely insignificant and meaningless matters. As William G. Sumner, Vilfredo Pareto, Graham Wallas, Harold Lasswell and many others have pointed out, people may feel that something is wrong but do not inevitably react in such a way as to solve those problems. They may, in the absence of proper training, react in any way which simply relieves tension.[9]

Following this line of thought, various social indices were examined in the hope of finding striking disparities between the behavior of Louisiana and that of other states. The results, however, were not striking. Louisiana ranked in the first quarter of the states in homicides and lynchings during the years 1918-1927.[10] In 1930, only South Carolina exceeded Louisiana in illiteracy. Over 7 per cent of the native Louisiana whites were illiterate and, since the whole scale of education is adjusted accordingly, there was also a high proportion of semi-literate persons. Together with Georgia, Louisiana was last among the southern states in the increase in average number of days attended by each pupil enrolled in 1920 and 1930.[11]

There are no data available on the number of civic organizations which mold public opinion in Louisiana. However, subjective estimates indicate that the number is too small for a healthy discussion of public issues. Some of the political organizations were by no means spontaneous, but arose at the instigation of some entrenched interest— political or economic. For example, the "Square Dealers" of 1935 were composed mainly of Standard Oil workers and discharged state employees. They drilled with firearms and for a time there was a general expectancy of a minor revolution.[12] The Constitutional League, formed by the "old gang politicians" to contest Longism and called by Long the "Constipational League," disbanded when he won the 1930 election.

The Louisiana newspapers do not have wide circulation in the hinterland. Hundreds of thousands of poor whites came to look to Huey P. Long for news and editorials, and his paper, which spoke their language, gained ever increasing prestige.[13]

John Stuart Mill once stated that the prerequisites for a republican form of government were: "(1) That the people should be willing to receive it. (2) That they should be willing and able to do what is necessary for its preservation. (3) That they should be willing and able to fulfill the duties and discharge the functions which it imposes on them.''[14] Louisiana satisfied none of these conditions.

The post-Civil War political leadership in Louisiana had never been capable of directing a bewildered and insecure population along progressive lines. The issues around which political opinion centered, however, are relatively discernible. Reconstruction left as destructive a blight upon Louisiana as on any other southern state.[15] Planters who had ruled before the Civil War were eventually restored to dignity and power. Gradually, however, they were dispossessed by the depression which settled over the entire South, losing bit by bit their old economic preeminence. Pressed by economic insecurity and born to rule, they maintained their command over southern politics long after their ideas had become stagnant and their philosophy moribund. Their slogans were outworn, their conventions were absurd, their respectability became pomposity. But new forces were at work in Louisiana. Yankees had come in to exploit its resources. New Orleans attracted gamblers and gangsters whose urbanizing influences cannot be overlooked. The city acquired a political machine similar to its northern prototypes. Louisiana, too, had a Tammany Hall. Dying aristocracy, however, held the state for a long time. In other southern states startling figures flashed on the political stage, heralds of new orders. For example, ''Pitchfork Ben'' Tillman, (1847-1918) of South Carolina, for many years agitated in Congress for the forgotten man in the South. But Louisiana was safe for the landed oligarchy and the new absentee industrial magnates until Huey Long entered the arena.

In the words of Howard W. Odum: ''The emerging picture is thus a logical one—the absence of economic issues in politics, the lack of experience and training in fiscal affairs, the political 'machine' politics of a Solid South, the dilemmas of modern issues to be attacked, and the whole question of the place of large race and propertyless classes in a region theoretically the most democratic in its clamor for the rights of the common man.''[16]

It is not enough to say that Louisiana gave birth to Long because the people were ignorant and corrupt. What types of ignorance and corruption produced the Long machine? At the risk of putting the cart before the horse, the answer will be sought by describing the Long machine at its peak, and then tracing its origin.

Long was at the peak of his power when he was assassinated by a political opponent on September 8, 1935. How he had consolidated his power after his election to the governorship in 1928, and what that power was may be summarized as follows:

The Governor, originally Long himself, and later one of his trusted lieutenants, had the right to call out the state militia without the interference of the courts.

The courts were deprived of all control over voting registration records.

The state administration had been given sole right to name polling booth commissioners.

All teachers and municipal employees were subject to state control and not to their respective local governments.

New Orleans had been deprived of revenues at the same time that its expenses were increasing, a situation which increased its dependence upon the state machine.

Baton Rouge Parish, once hostile to Long, had been made subject to him through the enactment of a law which gave the state administration the right to appoint enough police jurors from Long's adherents to overcome the anti-Long members who were popularly elected.

The city administration of Alexandria was legislated out of office.

Complete loyalty of all state employees to Huey Long was exacted.

A system which replenished campaign coffers through forced contributions of machine employees was enforced.

The legislature was at best a petty obstacle to Long—at worst a "rubber stamp."[17]

The Louisiana courts permitted an unusually broad interpretation of the police power, which enabled the state to interfere in many local affairs.

A plain-clothes state police responsible only to Long was powerful.

There is little indication that Long had any elaborate or well-thought-out social program. His "share-the-wealth" program had great appeal but little content.[18] His political and economic attitudes were as juvenile as Frank Hague's or Big Bill Thompson's. He loved the game of politics and played it for all it was worth, foregoing economic advantage in order to gain power.

The lack of any crystalized public opinion in Louisiana, noted above, is apparent from a study of election statistics. Fascism of the Italian and German sort presupposes highly conflicting and mutually exclusive parties contending for power. This was not so in Louisiana. Few people knew what was needed. They could only feel bitter. Long, unlike Mussolini or Hitler, was not forced into extreme reaction by the intensity of opposing social forces. Mass apathy enabled him to do what he wanted without violent opposition.

"Why," asked Raymond Gram Swing in 1935, "do these committee members take it lying down? . . . How can they put up with his bullying, his unsavory, blasphemous, overbearing language? They do not seem to be afraid of him; they appear to like him. Psychology explains the dictators of Europe as appealing to the innate yearning for father-authority in most people. But Huey is no father-figure. He is a grown-up bad boy."[19]

Why did Louisiana go as far as it did on the road to dictatorship? What part did the southern type of party system play? In the first place, where public opinion makes no demands, the legislators, accustomed to inactivity and job politics, can more readily adjust themselves to an executive who does all the planning and acting. In the second place, by virtue of being a one-party state, Louisiana could not very readily participate in the economic battles of national politics. Possibly the democratic primary might raise a class issue, but state politics, *in themselves*, are nowadays singularly free from major issues. Whereas a northern voter may have two chances to sift out a desirable candidate, the southern voter has only one, except in a run-off primary election.

It is proper to distinguish between that which has been ascribed to Long and that which is justifiably attributable to him. Some maintain that Long made use of economic appeals to a considerable extent, on the other hand, there are those who assert that he did not use economic symbols to the extent often reported.

The commentaries on Long show a general belief that he appealed to the poor whites of northern Louisiana and gradually to all the downtrodden people of the state. Judging from his many speeches, Long was acutely conscious of economic conflicts and reveled in old-fashioned Populist anti-corporation slogans. His declamations about the inequalities of educational opportunities show a certain sensitivity to some types of social injustice. His pleas against poll taxes were also an appeal to the poor man. But he was by no means an advocate of the right of labor to organize. One of his major lieutenants was a violent anti-unionist. Consistency in such matters may be foolish politics.

Long was, then, partially a reformer and partially a cynical politician. He evidently used economic symbols because they sounded good to him and because they worked. But they didn't bind him. Carleton Beals has commended that "Hard as Huey hammered the special interests, he was not averse . . . to take their money and aid if offered."[20] An astute analyst of the southern mind, W. J. Cash, said of Long:

> In his jesting humor, in his dealings with the skeptical tribe of reporters, he often delighted, indeed, to represent himself as simply a brazen master-manipulator at the calculus of demagoguery. And he never let his sentiment and his vision get in his way when any question of practical politics or boodle was at stake. Nevertheless, if you look into his serious deliverances, it is hard to avoid the sense that there was in him an almost wistful conviction that he was the destined liberator of the people who shouted after his car.[21]

Long was conscious and proud of his cynicism. He said of one of his legislators, "I bought him like a sack of potatoes." He would switch from pajamas to night-shirt in order to be photographed for his hill-billy constitutents. In southern Louisiana, so the story goes, he would say, "I don't drink" with a leer and wink; in northern

Louisiana the same statement was made with a stern and pious look. He gathered his strength in 1924 from the northern dry Baptists, and campaigned in 1926 for Edwin S. Broussard, a southern wet Catholic. If a man of principle is to be distinguished by the men with whom he refuses to keep company, Long had no principles, for he accepted any man or organization if it suited his purposes. Because he was full of sound and fury, he was regarded as more of a dictator than he actually was. He was frequently at odds with the press because it painted him in the black colors and compared him with Hitler and Mussolini. When all is said and done, however, Long was more of a master organizer and machine politician than a force particularly destructive of human values.

The Rise of Huey Long

Long had barely reached the eligible age of thirty when he decided to run for governor in 1924.[22] He was practically without organized support, but had benefited by some good publicity on the Public Service Commission to which he had been elected in 1918. Running as a dark horse, he was determined to give the other two Democratic candidates, Hewitt Bouanchaud, supported by the state machine, and Henry Fuqua, supported by the New Orleans city ring, stiff competition. Despite heavy rains which made country roads impassable for many of his constitutents, Long beat both of his opponents in the primary vote outside of New Orleans. But the city vote threw him out of the race and Fuqua won the run-off election.

The issues of the primary of 1924 were varied: The Ku Klux Klan pitted the northern section of the state, where it flourished, against the southern section, where Catholics predominated. Huey straddled the issue as best he could and refused to commit himself on the abolition of the Klan. Instead he introduced novel ideas and issues into the campaign. He attacked high taxes and demanded their abolition. He promised to disband the Conservation Commission and permit poor country folk to fish and hunt without charge. He attacked the large corporations as oppressors of the poor man. He advocated free school books and a concrete highway system-throughout the state.

And he seldom missed an opportunity to attack his opponents with unprecedented viciousness.

His organization support was practically negligible. His greatest asset was his contacts with the people, on whose doors he had knocked as a young salesman, and to whom he and his wife mailed campaign circulars. His superb evangelism and campaign oratory, added to his early experience and "common touch," constituted a formidable political weapon among the illiterate and backward country folk. The final count in the 1924 primary testifies to the effectiveness of these methods and Long never changed them. It is important to note that in this first campaign Long did not resort to the ingenious and fraudulent voting practices which later became part of his technique. As a result of his showing in this election, many political opportunists jumped on his bandwagon and the beginnings of a powerful machine were created.

The French parishes of southern Louisiana where Long received few votes in the 1924 primary, were predominantly Catholic, and very much in favor of repeal. The northern part of the state, Long's main support, was predominantly Protestant, anti-Catholic, and staunchly prohibitionist. The cleavage between Long's country and city votes was more clear cut than that between his northern and southern votes.

Maps and scatter diagrams are somewhat helpful in determining from what social groups Huey Long drew his main strength in 1924. The absence of relationship between the vote for Long and that of later elections in which he or his henchmen were candidates, indicates the lack of a machine in the first Long election; this lack soon disappeared. There was likewise no high degree of inverse relationship for his opponents in 1924. Joseph Ransdell, who was supported by Long in the senatorial campaign of 1924, did well in many parishes where Long ran poorly and vice versa. This is explained by the fact that Ransdell was the choice of the state machine. He was, moreover, a traditional ornament in state politics, having been senator for many years.

Maps and charts are not sufficient to show a relationship between

Longism and the vote of the low income classes, despite the statements that Long was the poor man's candidate. There are poor parishes in the south of Louisiana as well as the north, and here the rumors of Long's attachments to the Klan and his Protestant dry background nullified the effects of economic deprivations. A more thorough technique is necessary to make allowance for the Catholic vote. This might show a definite tendency for the poverty of the parish to be a strong factor in explaining its attachment to Long.[23] Long was a smart politician. He realized that his support from the northern country parishes was loyal but limited. He had to win the south and the machine in order to control the state.

In 1926, Edwin S. Broussard, a Creole Catholic from the South, sought re-election to the United States Senate on a wet repeal platform and was opposed by a Protestant dry. Long, a Baptist dry, gave Broussard a rousing support that won the primary election for him and the affection of many French voters. The anomaly of the combination is shown in the scatter diagram of the Long primary vote in 1924 and the Broussard primary vote in 1926. There is a slight inverse relationship, showing that where Broussard was weakest, Long was strongest.

In the 1928 primary, when Long again ran for governor, the northern and southern parishes gave him enough votes to defeat the New Orleans' machine candidate, Congressman Riley Wilson.[24] Lieutenant-Governor O. H. Simpson ran with the support of the state machine. Though again he lost New Orleans, Long carried the rural parishes by a landslide in the first balloting, and, although short of a majority, was so likely to get it that the opposition collapsed. Simpson decided to support Long, and Wilson withdrew from the race. This automatically insured Long's election as governor.

What do the scatter diagrams show for this primary election? As might be expected, there is no close relationship between the Long vote in 1924 and vote in 1928. Long had gained the support of new elements in the population. For example, Cameron and Evangeline parishes in the southern part of the state, which had given him 14 per cent and 13 per cent of their votes respectively in 1924, now gave

him 74 per cent and 73 per cent. These are extreme shifts, however.
There is no close relationship between Long's primary votes and economic status by parishes since he now had a majority in both poor
and rich French parishes.

Long had been consolidating his popular forces between 1924 and
1928. Now, as governor, he began to build his machine. He immediately forced the passage of bills allowing him large funds which he
could use for political purposes. When he called a special session of
the legislature to impose a tax on oil, impeachment proceedings were
begun against him, backed by Standard Oil and other business interests. By clever manipulation of faithful Senators, Long beat the
charges and promptly struck back. He succeeded in removing a number of state employees who had seemed unfriendly during the impeachment proceedings. He spent millions on highway construction
in a manner that favored his friends and punished his enemies. He
doled out payments in little strips to the parishes which pleased him.

In other state studies it has been possible to compare the voting
figures in the final elections of Democratic or Republican candidates
with the figures for the presidential candidates in that state. The
one-party system in Louisiana makes such comparisons difficult, since
everyone unites after the primary in support of the Democratic presidential candidate. But, though significant relationships between primary candidates and the Democratic presidential candidates cannot be
expected, there may be significant likenesses between the vote for candidates of the same faction at the different primary elections. A
study of such relationships in the 1920 Illinois Republican primary[25]
showed that one of the Republican candidates for senator, Frank L.
Smith, had profited to a great extent from the support of the Thomp-
son-Lundin-Small machine and that consequently there was a very
close connection in almost every county and Chicago ward between the
size of Smith's vote and that of Thompson for mayor in 1918 and
Small for governor in 1920. However, there was less of a relationship
between the Smith votes for 1920 and 1926. When Small's vote for
governor in the 1920 primary is compared with his votes in 1924
and 1928, a somewhat closer voting tradition is apparent.

How does Louisiana compare with Illinois? There was no relation-ship between the Long and Ransdell votes in 1924 or between the Long vote in 1924 and the Broussard vote in 1926, although Long sup-ported both of these candidates. There was only a slight similarity between the Long vote of 1930 and the vote for O. K. Allen for gov-ernor in 1932, although Allen was closely tied to Long. It may, there-fore, be concluded that Huey Long had to start with hardly any or-ganization and that he had to bargain as he went along, consolidating his gains until he built up a strong state-wide machine. Thus the similarity between the source of Long's vote in 1928 and in 1930 is noticeable, but there is no association of his vote with any social and economic groupings in the state—at least none that can be isolated through census data. His opposition can be isolated only in terms of personalities and interests; it is known, for example, that much of the opposition to Long in Caddo Parish and East Baton Rouge came from the Standard Oil Company.

Two things are striking about Louisiana politics during Long's political life. First, Long's support was mostly a personal endorse-ment and not support of his program of social reform. Most of his running mates in 1928 lost though Long himself won.[26] Secondly, Long's candidates in separate elections and his machine candidates during his entire hegemony could not count on a strictly "Long ma-jority" in the population.[27] This seems to indicate that Louisiana politics were based on "bread and butter" patronage and not long-term issues. A constantly shifting base of support showed that local machines were very active and supported no one who would not literally support them.

In most of the scatter diagrams on the Louisiana primary cam-paigns extreme variations appear from one election to another in a number of counties. People do not change their long-term political and economic views as rapidly as the diagrams indicate. The most powerful single factor, therefore, in those great changes was the parish machine. It distorts the picture which would perhaps other-wise be drawn by economic factors. This tendency becomes more evident when we remember that political machines are generally

stronger in the low income than in the high income parishes.   Other
evidence of the machine's power is in the manner in which the parish
votes are clustered.   For example, whereas in the Long election of
1924 only three parishes are located anywhere near the mean of the
distribution, seventeen parishes are below 15 per cent and twelve are
above 65 per cent.   Ordinarily the greatest cluster of county (parish)
votes centers around the median point.   But the machine in any parish
is either for or against a candidate, and if its power is strong, the
parish will be strongly for or against the candidate.   Another possibility is that great issues may have split the localities into quite opposite camps.   But the votes for Ransdell in 1924 and Broussard in
1926 also had high variations and yet they never represented live issues.   Consequently it is inescapable that the local machine was the key
to the problem.   As might be expected, the distribution was more
nearly normal in the presidential elections.

Later elections showed a more normal distribution.   This is partially accounted for by the growth of the Long machine which gained
control of the parish machines and caused a general uniformity in
parish voting behavior.   In the primary elections, whether northern
or southern, the relationship between candidates of the same faction
tended not to be as close as in the final election.[28] Deals were made by
the candidates with the localities and there were hardly any issues
to hold support over any period of time.   Only a rare man like Huey
Long could introduce enough discipline into local machines to guaran-
tee their loyalty.   Long was creating a real dynasty just before he
was assassinated, and his followers carried on with a machine stronger
that any he had ever had.   They were tied closely together in popular
support.   There was a fairly close relationship between the vote for
O. K. Allen for governor in 1932 and in 1936, though not as close
what might be expected.   The votes for John H. Overton for governor
in 1932, A. J. Ellender for senator, Richard W. Leche for governor
in 1936, and Earl Long in February, 1940, were similar in many
parishes, although local machines deserted the state machine for various reasons.   The 1936 primary elections in Louisiana offer an
example of machine and factional cohesion that is unparalleled in ex-

isting studies of American voting behavior. There was almost a perfect relationship in that year between the votes for Leche, Ellender,
and Allen, each drawing his strength in almost the exact proportion
from the individual parishes. Huey Long left an amazingly well-
disciplined machine. Unfortunately, only a governor was elected in
1940, so that it is impossible to ascertain whether there were great
changes in the Long organization between 1936 and 1940.

The conclusion, as it affects the American party system, becomes
evident. Important issues rarely touch the primaries. In a state
without significant final elections the electoral system contributes to
the degeneration of public opinion and the frustration of rational
politics. The one-party system and the economic and social problems
of Louisiana seem to complement each other.

It is a striking fact, apparent from a study of the election returns,
that the same type of southern political party system which fostered
the evasion of issues and the building of a strong personal government, also limited the cohesive powers of the machine over a period of
time. That there was little relationship between Long's vote in 1924
and in later elections and a high cohesion among the later Long machine candidates and himself, was expected. However, there was also
less relationship between members of the machine and Long than was
found between candidates of the same machine in northern states in
the final elections. The reasons for such an occurrence are: (1)
A low crystallization of public opinion, as indicated above; (2) the
fact that most voters in Louisiana are Democrat and therefore can
move easily from one faction of the party to another. There are no
legal or psychological barriers to changing loyalties—no party tradition; no strain on a life-long Republican who tries to become a
Democrat; no obstacles to national political alignments; no differences
as substantial as those between Democrats and Republicans in the
North; and finally, no single party machine which endures over a
number of years. By 1936, the Long machine had become complete
master of the state, but still these underlying factors made the foun-
dations of the machine insecure.

There is little doubt that the local politicians in Louisiana had strong machines in the parishes and could divert, in many cases, a commanding number of votes by shifting personal allegiances. An illustration or two may suffice. Orleans Parish, which contains mainly the city of New Orleans, has long been under the domination of a kind of Tammany Hall. Long was opposed from the outset of his career by the "Old Regulars" of the city. Notwithstanding his general motto, "If you can't lick 'em, join 'em!" Long was unable to break the hold of the machine on New Orleans with all its spoils and votes. In 1924, he received 18 per cent of the city's primary vote, in 1928, 23 per cent; and in 1930, 47 per cent. The marked change between 1928 and 1930 was not caused by the surrender of the machine. It still fought bitterly, but Huey controlled the state machine and manipulated it ingeniously. His agile mind conceived of much devilment. He waged open warfare against "lying newspapers," and his "sonofabitch" book, which contained the names of enemies marked for future retribution, grew ragged with use. State highway funds went only to supporters. Robert Maestri, New Orleans business man who was one of Huey's earliest backers, ended up as mayor. Huey wrested jobs from city control, ranted against the "evil metropolis" and used the militia to raid gambling houses. He resorted to the device of increasing state functions and thereby state patronage inside the city; for example, the Dock Board was granted additional funds for public works. Using the legislature's constitutional prerogatives and his own semi-legal or illegal devices, he showed the New Orleans machine by the vote of 1930 that it must either join him or be dissolved. It made its peace with Huey and has remained loyal to the Long machine up to the present time.[29]

On the other hand, Caddo Parish, located in the extreme northwestern part of the state and containing the city of Shreveport, was consistently opposed to Long, giving him 40 per cent of its votes in 1924, 39 per cent in 1928, and 41 per cent in 1930. The main-spring of the anti-Long forces there was the Standard Oil Company which maintained large fields and refineries in the region; the mayor of Shreveport was also a bitter opponent of Long. Standard Oil alternately made peace with and waged war against Long, who was not so much hostile to the company as he was unreliable. The successors of Long made peace with the company and captured the parish, but Sam Jones was favorable to the business interests and took the parish away from the machine in 1940.

Long was assassinated in 1935 and a group of less skillful politicians inherited his domain. They prospered for years under his lingering shadow, until they were decimated by a federal prosecutor and internal dissension. An orator at Huey Long's funeral had drawn the future with great intuition: "To you, the officials of state, the companions of political strategy, crusaders in a common cause, count memorable the day you first heard mention of his name. The time will come when to say that you even touched his hand will be the most potent interest in your life." For four years after Huey's death, the men who divided his leadership had little to fear and much to enjoy. In 1936, Allen was elected governor and Ellender and Leche senators with greater majorities than were ever given to Long. It was a rash man who dared to criticize the martyred Huey. His name mingled with that of the patron saints on the lips of the Cajun child at his nightly prayers.

Significant changes occurred, however, in the character of the machine. None of the masters bore the stamp of the avenging angel peculiar to Huey. In consequence, and not because the new bosses had less power than Huey, the press and the nation ceased talking about the Louisiana dictatorship. The bases of their support should be noted. While Huey rode to power on the back of the northern parishes, the popularity of his successors depended more and more on the New Orleans machine.[30] As rumor and gossip reached the hinterlands of the Babylonian practices in the old witch city, the popularity of Huey's henchmen declined. External conditions were little changed in the state. More grafting was done by state officials; less roads were built; and the new leaders were pale reflections of the dead genius. The general population felt that government was not entirely pure and decent in their state, but public lethargy needed more than a few ills to dissipate it. The state administration entrenched itself with the powers inherited from Long. It controlled election practices and administration, assessments, and even the courts. It used state jobs, paving contracts, and free school books as Huey taught it to use them. What ultimately destroyed the machine was its own crudity, its avarice, and a dogged and brilliant federal prosecutor.[31]

When indictments of state officials began, there was a kind of popular uprising. The reputable business men and civic leaders, middle class citizens who had never become quite acclimated to the rowdy Long type of government, moved in the direction of reform. Their representative, Sam Houston Jones, a lawyer from Cameron Parish ran for governor in January, 1940 on a platform to re-establish democratic government in Louisiana, though of course, at the same time to respect "all the good that Huey did."[32] He was opposed by Earl Long, Huey's brother, who promised to clean house if re-elected, and by James A. Noe, a disgruntled member of the Long machine. In the election, Long forged slightly ahead of Jones, with Noe a poor third, but when Noe threw his support to Jones, Long lost the run-off. A new regime was "in." But the basic conditions for desultory democracy remain. Unless Jones shows hitherto unrevealed powers, or unless a Huey Long with greater consistency and less cynicism arises, Louisiana democracy will function only feebly.[33]

LOUISIANA—PERCENTAGE FOR HUEY LONG OF TOTAL
VOTE FOR GOVERNOR, JANUARY, 1924

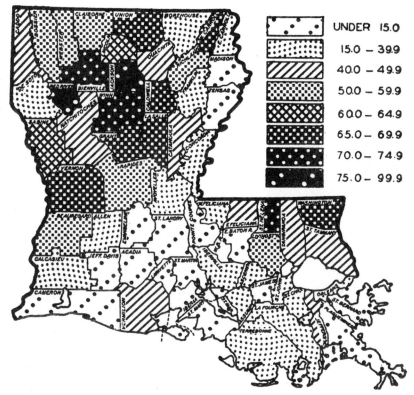

Figure 16

LOUISIANA—PERCENTAGE FOR EARL LONG OF TOTAL VOTE FOR
GOVERNOR, FEBRUARY, 1940

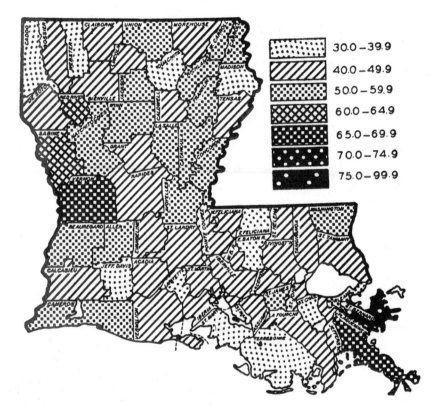

Figure 17

CHAPTER IX

THE FUTURE OF THE PARTY SYSTEM

THE NADIR of the democratic party system has been reached by the world. Never has factionalism been in such disrepute. Where it has not been rooted out by a painstaking and violent procedure, it has been frowned upon as a source of national disunity. Crisis is the keynote of our times and the minds of men do not run in gentle and tolerant channels.

To rid oneself of wishfulness and to analyze a complex situation in a complex world are tasks which seem unsurmountable. The most that can be done is to describe the major alternatives facing the world in the next few years, and to depict the party system which is most likely to fit each alternative.

The fate of parties in America will, of course, depend upon whether the war is short and not so costly, upon whether the war is long, bloody, and costly even though victorious, or upon whether we will lose the war through appeasement or defeat on the field of battle. If the war is not long and costly, we can expect a somewhat accelerated development of the peacetime trend which has been going on now for some years. If the war can be won without the loss of many American lives and too great a dislocation of American economic life, so much more gradual will be the American political process. The main transformations then will probably be (1) a catalytic effect on the processes of governmental and industrial centralization; (2) the appearance of parties divided more on economic and class lines; (3) the decline of the old type of patronage system with the consequent appearance of the problem of neutralization of the bureaucracy; and (4) a shift in functions of the local civic groups in conjunction with the changing character of municipal politics and the class cleavages mentioned above.

The number of those who foresee the doom of democracy in the increased collectivism of the federal government and in the increasing number of government employees is only equaled by the number of those who see in this trend the salvation of democracy. Probably, the question as to who is right is incidental to the question as to who thinks he is right enough to fight about it. The party in power, if the examples of history serve us right, would not be inclined to use violence instead of the legal means of change within its possession. But those employers who have used strikebreakers in the past have the psychology necessary for breaking up the legal processes of state, and their wrath would feed on the reaction of government and labor to their activities.

Those who view the increasing governmentalization of our life as hostile to democracy are unimpeachedly democratic in some cases, outright fascist in others. Both identify democracy with the unrestrained capitalistic era. While Walter Lippmann sees in planning the death of the freedoms and therefore decries it, Lawrence Dennis sees planning as inevitable and therefore considers Fascism as necessary and desirable. "The very essence of the concept of planning," according to Lippmann, "is that a design can be adopted to which people will thereafter conform. This is equivalent to saying that a democratic people cannot have a planned economy."[1] Dennis asserts: "Successful technology requires empirical truth. Successful political democracy seemingly requires persuasive lies. Sometimes these lies are called idealism; the most favorable description of them to accord with the facts is to call them utopian fictions or myths. But you cannot run a complex machine by myths and fictions even of the law."[2]

The conclusion is inescapable that there must be planning in the short run at least. All-out war production involves huge debts, the regulation of prices, the rationing of some goods, and these controls cannot be relaxed immediately upon the cessation of hostilities. Plans for the immediate future inevitably include reconstruction. Those who see in these measures the decline of democracy have reason to be content with the great degree of freedom permitted within this system as compared with other systems. It may help their peace of mind if they are able to see the increase in planning not as a temporary imposition of restraints on the minority by a despotic and transient majority, but as a development of the "state ways" (folkways) of a society. Then it would appear clearer to them that a political democracy rests on basic sentiments, that no society is ever completely free, and that freedom exists in terms of certain areas where choices may be made without disrupting the fabric of society. The future of the American party system depends not only on the preservation of the freedoms but also upon the building of national unity.

Studies of voting behavior made by psychologists, sociologists, journalists, political scientists, and public opinion analysts tend to show that the American party system is undergoing some radical changes. While sectional, religious, and traditional influences are still important in national politics and tend to produce political behavior independent of economic considerations, yet analysis shows that more and more the two major parties are dividing on the basis of income groupings. The Democratic party is becoming the party of the lower income groups—the organized industrial workers and the beneficiaries of the relief, farm, housing, lending and other programs of the national government. The Republican party, on the other hand, is tending to become a party of the higher income groups—the business-men, the professional classes, white-collar workers, and the independent farmers who have not felt that they have benefited from the farm programs.

The recent findings of research workers in the field of American politics show that the trend toward the agreement of political and economic divisions is still offset by many counter-influences. In the South, the Democratic party remains the party of the upper income groups and the social elite. On the other hand, in the North there are many people in the lowest income groups who vote the Republican ticket. Negroes in domestic service or in independent employments, unskilled laborers whose precarious tenure depends upon business conditions,[3] small independent farmers situated on poor soil, and poorly paid white-collar workers who take pride in their middle-class standing still support the Republican party in large numbers. Studies of voting behavior which are based on the official election returns do not shed direct light upon this trend; the different income groups within a given country are lumped together and the variations in their voting habits are concealed. If, however, the voters tended to concentrate in certain areas on the basis of income and if the voting records for those areas were available, the official election returns would be unusually useful. Litchfield's analysis of Detroit,[4] the writer's studies of Chicago,[5] and the preceding chapters show that the relationship of political and economic alignments may be studied in this fashion.

While the trend toward class division in American politics became marked during the thirties, it was not an entirely new phenomenon. In the election of 1896 may be found many antecedents of the 1940 alignment. William Jennings Bryan, the Democratic candidate, appealed to the farmers in the West and the laborers in the cities, while his Republican opponent, William McKinley, had the support of the upper income groups, the professional classes and those who felt that their welfare depended upon the success of the wealthy. Under the skillful guidance of his campaign manager, Mark Hanna, a successful businessman, McKinley won a sufficiently large number of the middle and lower income groups to carry the election, but it is entirely probable that if Bryan had had the same facilities to carry his message to the lower income groups that McKinley enjoyed, the results might have been different. In 1896 the country was deluged with printed propaganda for the Republican cause, while Bryan, a tireless speaker, had time to reach but a small fraction of the masses. If the radio had been in as wide use in 1896 as in 1940, Bryan would have had a more even chance.

In this connection it is worthy of note that President Franklin D. Roosevelt's training in national politics came during the Wilson administration. In 1912 Wilson barely held the Bryan vote and he won out principally because of the split in the Republican party. In 1916, however, Wilson built up a popular constituency among the farmers of the West and South and the workers in some of the eastern centers.

The trend toward an income group cleavage in American politics appeared again in the presidential election of 1924. In that year the influence was marked in the Republican party, but not very clearly in the Democratic. La Follette's Progressive party support came from the ranks of organized labor and some of the liberal-minded farmers in the Middle West. Calvin Coolidge received the traditional Republican vote which included the upper income level in the North. On the other hand John W. Davis, who received the lowest vote cast for any Democratic candidate since the Civil War, drew his supporters from the foreign-born elements in the metropolitan centers and the die-hards in the South, the border states and certain parts of the North. Some began to predict that the Democratic party would disappear,[6] failing to see the possibilities of a rejuvenation of the Democratic party by a combination of the Progressive and old-line Democratic elements.

In 1928 Alfred Smith began the process of bringing the labor elements into the Democratic party. In the big cities of the North, particularly in those which had a considerable number of Catholics, he made an excellent showing.[7] If organized labor had been as strong in Pennsylvania and New York, Illinois and Ohio in 1928 as it was in 1940, Smith might have come close to winning, in spite of the defection of the traditional Democrats in the South.

In the Roosevelt elections of 1932, 1936 and 1940, there was a general shift in party alignments. While many wealthy persons who had heavy losses in the downward spiral of the business cycle voted against hard times and Hoover in 1932, they were back in the Republican fold by 1936. However, that election swept away large portions of the lower income strata support which the Republican party had had in the first part of the twentieth century. Gone was the patronage base, gone was the whip hand in the former employer-controlled counties,[8] gone was the almost universal conviction of the Negroes that they must support the Republican party at all costs, and gone was the widespread belief among many working class people that their interests were identified with the interests of the wealthy classes.

An examination of recent party platforms will not reveal any increasing economic group antagonism in American politics. It might be said that one of the characteristics of the political process in the United States has been the repression of fundamental issues by the major party spokesmen. For instance, in the presidential campaign just eight years before the Civil War, one looks in vain for a stand by a major party leader on the burning issues of slavery and secession. The old Whig party dissolved rather than face this issue. Again in 1916 the United States faced a fundamental issue, namely what would be the role of this country in world affairs. During the campaign, neither of the major party candidates had the courage to take a definite stand on this question. President Roosevelt has likewise been unwilling to indicate all of the implications of his New Deal program and his opponents have been unwilling to denounce any significant portion of that program. But shadow-boxing does not fool the great mass of the voters. Landon and Willkie might give lip service to organized labor, the troubles of the unemployed, the problems of the farmers, but it appeared to these groups that the backers of the Republican candidates were not sympathetic toward their cause. "While the Republican party organization man seems to roost on the voter's doorstep, the amazing Roosevelt has become one of the family." That view was expressed by a Republican precinct captain.[9]

The popular basis of the New Deal victories is not the same as that of the Wilson victories, Roosevelt was able to obtain such strong support in the North and the West that it was not necessary for him to depend as much upon the conservatives of the South as President Wilson was compelled to do.

While the trend toward a more sharply defined economic division has been unmistakable, it has not endangered the democratic system from within. One general proposition which political theorists have agreed upon is that our democratic system is based upon a consensus of fundamental political ideas and when this consensus is lacking, the democratic process breaks down. In the United States this occurred in the campaign of 1860. Not since the Civil War has there been any election after which there was not sufficient ground for agreement between the major parties so that economic activities could continue as usual. The existence of such national unity has meant that it has been safe for candidates to talk about fundamental issues with the realization that there were no basic cleavages separating them from the opposition. William Jennings Bryan in the Democratic campaign of 1896 talked about the battle of wage-earners and farmers against plutocracy, but after the election he did not urge any violent action against the opposing forces. It is significant to note that the Republican party in 1936 and 1940 carefully avoided any explicit references to economic cleavages and stressed the unity of the country behind the existing economic system. On the eve of the election, William Allen White said, "There is no great issue before the country to divide the people: man and man should dwell in unity."[10] Bryan looked upon the election as the process of getting back to the accustomed ways of life, not as a revolutionary appeal.

The New Deal elections were more like the election of 1896 than that of 1860. Characteristic of American political campaigns has been the emphasis upon personalities. Willkie recognized this when he said, "The American people do not give their vote to policies; they give their vote to men who, in their opinion, will not let them down."[11]

Since 1860 there have been four complete cycles in American politics. At the beginning of each of these cycles the Democratic party was in power but in a position of declining influence. A cycle was completed when the Democrats came back to power. The beginning of 1942 found the United States in the fifth political cycle. Barring an international catastrophe with a resulting economic chaos, it is likely that the fortunes of the opposition party will rise again.

The old type of patronage politics has been declining. By the hundreds of thousands, governmental employees have been encompassed by civil service regulations. The federal service is in great part subject to merit considerations and the state and local government services increasingly so. The political machines of the future may face a scarcity of patronage to dispense, and the public may face a great body of governmental servants whose participation in politics would be a delicate matter to adjust. Professional party workers may be fewer, and more and more dependence on voluntary workers and organized groups may result. With an increased class antagonism, the labor unions and the employers' associations may be expected to take up an increased amount of the burden of supporting the parties.

But an unheralded and perhaps more significant change in the party structure will come about through the new positions which some party will fill in the bureaucracy. Initially, of course, the party in power will tend to offer appointments to men who believe in their dogmas. But as soon as they take office, political appointees begin to lose their former attachments and instead become attached to the system which furnishes them a living and a role in society. Once entrenched in office, they pursue certain collective goals. These are seldom the goals of the political system which existed before they took office, but those of the governmental system under which they work.

Concurrent with this trend in national politics is the tendency for nonpartisan and civic groups to become partisan. Civic organizations are today preponderantly middle class. Their aims are efficiency in government, elimination of corruption and bossism in politics, and the improvement of middle-class living standards. As the

national parties become more divided on the basis of income and social class, local groups will become divided along the same lines.
Simultaneously, economic classes tend to have fewer nonpartisan functions. James Burnham described this tendency in *The Managerial
Revolution:*

> The New Deal has further curbed the masses by tying the popular organiza-
> tions closer and closer to the state. This development is characteristic of the
> managerial revolution in all nations. It is strikingly illustrated in the United
> States by the history of the labor movement during the New Deal period. . . .
> The A. F. of L., as a result, is abandoning its traditional stand-off policy. More-
> over, the history of the New Deal relations with farmers' and consumers' or-
> ganizations parallels the labor movement tendencies. The examples of Russia
> and Germany have already taught us that the early forms of managerial society
> require fusion of the popular organizations with the state. The bureaucrats
> in charge of the popular mass organizations, in fact, take their place among the
> managers. This tendency, like the other managerial tendencies, is conspicuous
> in the New Deal.[12]

The precarious foundation of American democracy and the two-
party system is clearly shown by the events of the past twenty years
in the state of Louisiana and the urban community of Jersey City.[13]
In these two widely scattered jurisdictions, we have seen the rise of
a type of political control which bears some strong resemblances to
dictatorship. Huey Long at the peak of his power in 1935, and Mayor
Hague before he suffered some reverses in the courts, controlled the
political affairs of their respective bailiwicks with a blatant dema-
goguery, ruthlessness and utter disregard of the democratic process.
Opposition parties were intimidated, freedom of speech was practically suspended and the full financial powers of the respective
governments were used to place the citizens under no obligation
to men who, in common parlance, would probably be termed "bosses"
rather than dictators. But the citizens of Louisiana and of Jersey City
did not rise up and fight for their basic democratic freedoms. They
were apparently content with their lot. Chapter VIII indicates that
upon his death, the "Kingfish" became a legendary hero of the voters
of his state. "Boss" Hague's power has not to date been successfully challenged in his own city.

What happened in Louisiana and Jersey City might happen in the United States as a whole if the economic system developed serious maladjustments and men arose to exploit them.

Fortunately, the seeds of totalitarianism which have been sowed in this country have not been very fruitful. The Communist party, acting in accordance with the dictates of the Third International, has never found favor with the American electorate. Even in the crisis election of 1932 its vote was insignificant.[14] On the other hand, throughout American history intolerant, strong-armed organizations have continued to come into existence. The Know-Nothing party of the fifties, the Ku Klux Klan of the Reconstruction days, the Klan of the post-Versailles days, and the various shirt organizations of the thirties (the Silver Shirts, the Khaki Shirts, the White Shirts, the Black Shirts, the Brown Shirts, and the Blue Shirts) show that there is an incipient Fascism in the United States ready to flare up when conditions are favorable.[15] While these fascist-like organizations have not gained any permanent ground, it is important to note that the rapid multiplication of such movements shows that there is here a potential menace to the American democracy. A sharp turn for the worse in the international situation or in the economic cycle might furnish an opportunity for an American *Fuehrer*.

Another index of the insecurity of American democracy may be found in repressive legislation affecting informal, unlawful groups. Such legislation has precedents antedating the Civil War. The Anti-loyalist laws, the Alien and Sedition laws of 1798, the suspension of writ of habeas corpus during the Civil War, the Federal Espionage law and the state sedition acts during World War I, and the post-war criminal syndicalist, anti-anarchists, anti-sabotage laws are examples of this type of legislation. Mention should also be made of the growth of laws which exclude the Communist party from the ballot (one of Hitler's first acts was the exclusion of the Communist party). Sometimes old statutory and common-law devices of repression are employed in connection with riots, breaches of peace, manifestations of disorderly conduct, and public meetings.

The last decade has raised a whole series of questions regarding the faith of the American people in the possible solution of their difficulties by the democratic process. With increasing frequency, organized farmers, unionized workers, and business organizations have used violence to accomplish their purposes. Milo Reno and the Farm Holiday Association defied the regular processes of foreclosure. Potentially, the sit-down strikes might have developed violence of the type found in Italy in 1919-22 just prior to Mussolini's coming to power. La Follette's investigation of the strong-arm tactics of business showed the dangers in this direction.[16]

An outstanding characteristic of the totalitarian regime is the use of violence by government to settle disputes which, under a democracy, are decided by the peaceful process of compromise. During the disturbing years of the depression, there was a tendency for state governments to use militia and the National Guard—as in Oklahoma, Indiana, Ohio and Rhode Island. Often the action taken has been illegal and on a number of occasions it has been restricted by Federal Court injunction. Should the conduct of the war be imperilled, it is likely that further repressive measures would be employed to end strikes and industrial sabotage and curb fomenters of disunity.

If Germany wins the war, if there is a negotiated peace, or if we win after a terrible struggle, the results may be similar. The anti-liberal, anti-revolutionary, and anti-democratic elements in the nation would probably be immeasurably strengthened. The prestige of democracy might be destroyed. The insecurities of the post-war epoch may bring about great irrational outbursts. Fascists are masters. A prolonged and exhausting war would leave so great a trauma that any system affected by it might be visited by disaster afterwards.

In America, the pre-Pearl Harbor group known as "America First" contained within itself most of the formerly overt fascistic organizations in the United States. By specific command, the members of the German Bund and other fascist groups joined "America First." From it, they obtained respectability, converts, and protection. In return, they infected it with anti-semitism and anti-liberalism. For the first time in American history a mass basis of miscellaneous social and political elements was built around a common dread of war.

The reason for Americans' tolerance of political differences in the past was a sort of political indifference as well as common agreement to tolerate disagreement. The basis for non-violence in politics (excluding occasional violence at the polls and the Civil War) has been in part a preoccupation with personalities and a disregard of, and aversion towards, politics. The future promises a more highly crystallized public opinion.

The democratic party system, based on a tolerance of conflicting views and interests, faces severe tests in the future. It must maintain a morale which can withstand the emotional strains following in the wake of continual crisis over a period of years. Traditional sources of morale are diminishing and strenuous steps should be taken to recruit the middle class on the side of the survival of the two-party system. This is difficult to do since the case of many sections of the middle class is depressing. Their lack of faith in the democratic way of life has been growing during the decade of the thirties and their very economic existence is being threatened by the economic controls of the present war period. Protestant ministers, whose sermons were printed in the *Christian Pulpit* between the years 1920 and 1941, turned completely around from a confidence in man's powers of reason, his need of freedom, and his good nature during the twenties, to a distrust of the ability of reason, an emphasis on the need and value of faith, a conviction of the necessity of discipline by the state, and a feeling that man is essentially evil. This was the trend of thought among those who both reflected and led the class which was formerly the basis for the American democracy—the middle class.

The future of the American party system depends upon our faith in the efficacy of the democratic process to solve the difficult problems of the war and post-war periods, upon our willingness to make sacrifices to attain national unity, upon our ability to achieve discipline without going fascist, and upon our tolerance of changes in our economic and political institutions urgently called for by the times.

METHODS OF STUDYING POLITICAL BEHAVIOR

AFTER several paragraphs of favorable comment, a recent reviewer of *Machine Politics* ended up by saying that it was possible to understand the book without commanding the whole battery of scientific techniques of modern social science. He went on to state that it was his impression that any other investigator of equal intelligence, industry, ingenuity and capacity for observation would have reached the same conclusions with the application of no mathematics higher than grade school arithmetic. In his opinion the principal value of techniques used in connection with this particular piece of research lay in the demonstration that the employment of these most highly refined methods for measuring and evaluating political data has yielded substantially, if not altogether, the same results as the employment of familiar tools at the command of every intelligent and moderately educated persons. Unfortunately, the reviewer did not distinguish between the familiar tools and scientific techniques.

In any investigation a primary problem is the collection of data. A twofold classification may be made of possible methods: first, the collection from official sources, such as election sources; and second, the collection of original data. In using data which are already collected there is great economy of effort but the hypotheses to be investigated are limited by influences outside the control of the investigator. Records by individual persons are rarely available and the investigator must rely upon central tendencies in areas. However, where voting records are obtainable they may be analyzed by simple tabulation as in the case of the Fearing study of Palo Alto, California, the Dennis study of Lansing, Michigan, the Martin study of Austin, Texas, the Dunkelberger study of five counties in Pennsylvania, the Pollock studies in Michigan, and the Chicago studies.

The familiar methods for collecting original data involve the use of schedules that contain items of a more or less objective type, such as those used by Arneson in his study of Delaware, Ohio, and many of those used by the public opinion surveys. It may also involve the collection of subjective data, such as the reasons for a particular type of political behavior. In the Chicago study of non-voting, the voters were asked why they failed to exercise the suffrage on a given occasion. Here the question may be raised as to how reliable are the reasons given. Are the reasons mere excuses or rationalizations? How accurately can the average voter state his motives? In the second Chicago study the reasons for not voting given by the non-voters taken from the control and experimental groups did not yield the expected distributions. While this finding is not conclusive, it might raise some doubts regarding the validity of answers given to such questions.

In trying to analyze subjective attitudes it is far superior to employ more systematic questionnaires such as the attitude scales worked out by Thurstone and his followers. Dr. Beyle has produced a very interesting scale of attitudes toward individual candidates.

The relatively simple methods so far discussed have involved little more than ordinary arithmetic. The analysis of large segments of political behavior must still proceed by qualitative methods. No reputable statistician calls for the exclusive use of quantitative methods. In the analysis of political behavior the case history, life history, the opinion of experts, the observations of participants and the familiar historical methods are still indispensable. While the sociologists have spent a great deal of time and energy in the perfection of the life-history technique, political scientists with the exception of several isolated pioneers such as Dr. Harold Lasswell, have largely neglected this very promising method. The opinion of experts is being employed to a growing extent by political scientists as the studies of J. T. Salter and others indicate. Raymond Moley in his recent book has shown some of the advantages to be gained by the participant-observer method.

Employed in *Machine Politics* and the present study are zero order correlations, simple regression equations, partial correlations, net regression equations, and factorial analysis using the centroid method developed by Professor Thurstone of the University of Chicago. I take it that these would be called by my reviewer refined statistical techniques.

The reviewer presented two interesting challenges to those persons who are interested in possible application of quantitative methods to the study of political behavior. What can be said about his propositions? Would the same conclusions have been reached with ordinary grade school arithmetic? Most certainly I hold no brief for the exclusive use of statistical methods. Quantitative methods may be used either to test significant hypotheses or to reveal relationships that require further exploration. I would not deny categorically the proposition of the reviewer. However, I would state emphatically that to prove the propositions stated in *Machine Politics* as conclusively using only grade school arithmetic would have required much more time and effort than I took. This may seem like a paradox to those who may not have familiarized themselves with the techniques, but once their use is learned it is soon discovered that they are great labor and space-saving devices. To have presented the evidence in as convincing a fashion without the use of statistics would have required a book five or six times as large. A scatter diagram takes a whole page. It is possible to present over 300 zero order coefficients of correlation on a single page. Here was a saving of over 300 pages alone. An equation of a net regression can be presented in a single line. Ezekiel in his *Methods of Correlation Analysis* takes an entire chapter to present graphical methods for determining how one variable changes when two or more other variables change. Furthermore, his graphical methods could not be used very readily in the Chicago study since there were 144 different units to analyze and the graphical method becomes altogether too complicated with such a large number of cases.

The reviewer further stated that the same results would have followed the employment of familiar tools. One chapter of *Machine Politics* is devoted to the analysis of the relationship of the press to voting in Chicago. In view of the fact that most of the Chicago daily newspapers were Republican in national politics, the common sense observation regarding the 1936 election was that the influence of the press was declining. It was said that the day when the journalist wielded great political power was over. The device of net correlation showed that this was not an accurate statement of the situation. After making allowance for some of the other influences related to voting behavior it was found that the net relationship of the press to party voting was still significant. To have demonstrated this in as clear a fashion by using merely the familiar tools would have required a very elaborate field analysis. One of the great labor-saving aspects of *Machine Politics* was its use of data collected by other agencies.

The proper use of the various labor-saving and time-saving devices is not easy. The ordinary books on statistics are clear enough on the mathematical derivation of the different formulae, but as a rule they are woefully inadequate in discussing the interpretation of the results obtained in given situations. Take such a result as a coefficient of a correlation. In the analysis of political behavior, the zero order coefficient of correlation by itself may or may not be meaningful. This was brought to my attention in a dramatic way in connection with an analysis of the accuracy of the straw polls. I discovered that the coefficient of correlation between the *Literary Digest* polls and the final election results was .91. Such a high coefficient would lead many educators to say that there was a very close relationship. However, everyone knows that the *Literary Digest* missed the election so badly that the magazine went out of existence. When one looks at the regression equation, then the coefficient takes on

more meaning.   A perfect prediction would have been one in which
for every state percentage of the *Literary Digest* poll you had a corresponding and equal state percentage in the final election result.
The generalized equation for a straight line is as follows: $Y = a + bX$,
where the constant a represents the intercept on the Y-axis and b represents the slope.   Let Y equal the final per cent for Roosevelt in 1936
by states.   Let X equal the per cent given to Roosevelt by the *Literary
Digest* poll by states.

If the *Literary Digest* had made a perfect prediction, the equation would have read: $Y = X$ in which the constant a would have
a value of zero and the constant b would have the value of one.   However, the actual equation obtained by the ordinary statistical methods
was as follows: $Y = 33 + .69X$.   It is clear from this equation that if
one knew in advance the exact nature of the bias in the *Literary Digest*
poll, he might have made a pretty good prediction.   The high coefficient of the correlation merely means that the deviations from the
line of best fit were not very great.   However, in this case the line
of best fit was some distance from the line of perfect prediction.
Another way of presenting this would be to say that the difference
between the two means was so large that the *Literary Digest* poll
could not be used to predict, even though it did give a rough rank
order of the states.   From this we may conclude that anyone who presents a coefficient of correlation without presenting the regression
equation or data from which it may be derived may be withholding
an essential part of the proof.   Correlational methods, properly used,
furnish one of the best methods of checking the accuracy of the polls.

The interpretation of equations of the net regression is even more
difficult.   For any function using more than three variables no simple
geometric or graphical representation is possible.   In an equation of
net regression as in simple correlation we are seeking the function of best fit for the data, that is, the combination of variables that
will best account for the variations in the variable which we wish
to explain.   There are two types of interpretation of an equation
of net regression.   First, it is said that the equation furnishes an
estimate of the values of a given dependent variable from the func-

tion of several independent variables. The second interpretation is that the equation gives an idea of the relative importance of each of the independent variables in accounting for the variation of the dependent variable. In interpreting such an equation it is said the relationship between the dependent variable and the single independent variable when all other factors are held constant is analyzed. The analogy of the controlled experiment is sometimes employed. This is misleading since net regression and partial correlation do not involve holding constant the *values* of a variable but only the *variations* which are attributed to any one variable.

Using these methods to study the 1936 presidential election returns in Iowa by counties, it was found that as compared with 1932 the bulk of the voters did not change their party affiliations. However, there were some shifts between the two elections and the greatest shifts away from Roosevelt were in the counties where the voters were predominantly dry, native white, and the farmers had suffered the greatest corn losses in the years 1935-1936. Roosevelt held his ground or gained in 1936 in those counties where there were large percentages of wet, foreign born, city dwellers and farmers who suffered relatively small losses in corn production.

Because of the difficulties involved in interpreting equations of net regression and coefficients of partial correlation and also because these correlation methods are not readily applicable to problems involving more than five or six variables, it is sometimes useful to employ factorial methods. In factor analysis we have a new device for presenting a series of relationships in a simplified fashion.

Factor methods were first devised to study the interrelationships between the psychological tests. The purpose of the method was to find how few tests needed to be used to isolate certain primary abilities. Or putting it in other terms, how few primary abilities it is necessary to postulate in order to explain a table of intercorrelations between test results. If two tests measure the same primary ability then one may be substituted for the other. Factor methods involve the examination of the whole battery of tests and the elimination of all unnecessary tests. It employs the methods of matrix algebra and vector analysis. Dr. Thurstone found that seven different scores contain essentially all the information given by fifty-six psychological tests. Geometrically speaking, this meant that, beginning with a fifty-six-dimensional space he found that the set of points tended to occupy a seven-dimensional space. This great reduction is of enormous value in the testing field.

Factor analysis may be employed in social science wherever one can construct a rectangular table (matrix). In voting problems each area may take the place of a person. In lieu of tests, information regarding different areas may be employed. It is then possible to determine whether or not a smaller number of variables serve equally well to describe the relationships.

In *Machine Politics* a table of over 300 coefficients of correlation may be presented as a simple diagram containing one point for each variable concerned. Factorial methods may be used to test a number of significant hypotheses. In the analyzing of political behavior these methods so far have been used in a preliminary fashion. Factor analysis merely takes the variables and sorts them into various related groups. All the variables within a single group are interrelated and hence may be regarded as different explanations of a more fundamental tendency. To the extent to which different variables are concerned with reflections of independent factors, partial correlation has no effect so that here the factorial methods have decided advantages.

Can the experimental methods be applied to the analysis of political problems? That question is frequently raised in the discussion of research methods in political science. Some years ago in my study, *Getting out the Vote,* I made an attempt to measure the influence of a nonpartisan canvass upon the size of the vote cast. In his analysis of this study, appearing in *Methods in Social Science,* Catlin stated that he thought the method might be called experimental if the study were successfully repeated. To my knowledge no repetition of this type of analysis has been made. However, many social psychologists have made studies which employed somewhat similar devices. The control and experimental groups can be roughly set up but the type of experimentation that can be done is limited.

In this brief summary I have tried to sketch some of the methods which may be used in studying political behavior. Because of the critical attitude taken by many political scientists toward the use of statistical methods, I have tried to point out some of the advantages to be gained by employing these methods. In addition to their value as labor-saving and time-saving devices, the quantitative techniques promise to give some very fruitful results if significant hypotheses and relevant indexes can be devised.

TABLES

I: PENNSYLVANIA ELECTION RETURNS AND DEMOCRATIC
PERCENTAGES, 1924-1940

	Votes in Thousands			Democratic Percentage for State	Democratic Percentages by Counties		
	Democrat[1]	Republican	Total		Mean	Lowest	Highest
President, 1924..	409	1,401	2,117[2]	19.3	24.6	9	54
Senator, 1926 ...	649[3]	822	1,471	44.1	57.5	19	76
President, 1928..	1,068	2,055	3,123	34.2	27.1	12	60
Senator, 1928	1,029	1,949	2,978	34.6	29.1	13	55
Governor, 1930..	1,010[4]	1,069[5]	2,079	48.6	38.6	19	76
Senator, 1930......	523	1,462	1,985	26.4	29.0	11	54
President, 1932..	1,296	1,454	2,750	47.1	45.7	24	66
Senator, 1932......	1,201	1,376[6]	2,577	46.7	45.3	24	67
Governor, 1934..	1,476	1,410	2,886	51.1	49.9	31	64
Senator, 1934....	1,494	1,367	2,861	52.2	50.6	31	65
President, 1936..	2,354	1,690	4,044	58.2	52.1	30	69
Senator, 1938......	1,694[7]	2,087	3,781	44.8	40.2	24	54
Governor, 1938..	1,756[8]	2,035	3,791	46.3	42.3	27	56
President, 1940..	2,171	1,890	4,061	53.5	46.7	27	64
Senator, 1940......	2,070	1,893	3,963	52.2	45.6	27	63

[1]"Democrat" is used where the majority of the candidate's votes are on the Democratic ticket; "Republican" where the majority of the candidate's votes are on the Republican ticket.
[2]Total includes vote for La Follette, candidate on the Socialist and Labor tickets. He received 307,000 votes.
[3]Includes 33,000 on Labor ticket.
[4]Includes 367,000 Liberal votes, and 462 Independent votes.
[5]Includes 32,000 votes on Prohibition ticket and 360 Independent votes.
[6]Includes 4,000 votes on Liberal ticket.
[7]Includes 10,000 votes on Royal Oak ticket and 74 Non-Partisan votes.
[8]Includes 11,000 votes on Royal Oak ticket, 59 Non-Partisan, and 8 no party.

II: SELECTED SOCIAL AND ECONOMIC VARIABLES FOR PENNSYLVANIA

Name	Value for State	Mean	σ	Range Low	High
Pro-Repeal, 1933	76.2	61.6	13.6	31	89
Rural-Farm Population, 1930	8.8	20.9	13.8	----	45
Native-White Population, 1930	82.6	73.0	16.7	35	98
Catholicity, 1926	22.0	14.6	11.1	----	46
Percentage of Population, WPA 1939	8.4	10.3	4.4	2	25
Percentage on Direct and Work Relief, 1936	----	12.9	5.4	5	28
Shift in Index Number, 1928-32 (n=65)[1]	—48.6	—46.9	+10.0	—69	—22
Shift in Index Number, 1932-36 (n=65)	+31.8	+33.7	+14.8	----	+67
Shift in Democratic Vote, 1928-32 (n=65)	+12.5	+18.8	+ 8.0	— 7	+34
Shift in Democratic Vote, 1932-36 (n=65)	+11.1	+ 6.2	+ 6.2	— 7	+19
Shift in Democratic Vote, 1936-38 (n=65)	—13.5	—11.5	+ 4.4	—23	— 2

[1]Cameron and Blair Counties eliminated from calculation of Means, σ, and Range in all the shifts.

III: VARIABLES RELATED TO VOTING BEHAVIOR IN PENNSYLVANIA, 1924-1940, CORRELATION MATRIX

Column legend (symbol = variable): a Pres. 1924; b Sen. 1926; c Pres. 1928; d Sen. 1928; e Gov. 1930; f Sen. 1930; g Pres. 1932; h Sen. 1932; i Gov. 1934; j Sen. 1934; k Pres. 1936; l Sen. 1938; m Pres. 1940; n Catholicity 1926; o Amendment #5 1933; p Pro-Repeal 1933; q Native White 1930; r Vote Shift 1936-1938; s Rural Farm 1930.

Name	Date	Sym	a	b	c	d	e	f	g	h	i	j	k	l	m	n	o	p	q	r	s
Pres.	1924	a		.53	.05	.29	.19	.66	.55	.58	.36	.32	.26				-.29				
Sen.	1926	b	.53		-.50	-.32	-.31	.16	.03	.17	.06	.03	-.20				-.66	-.67			
Pres.	1928	c	.05	-.50		.96	.48	.47	.68	.55	.52	.55	.60			.76	.48	.62	-.68		
Sen.	1928	d	.29	-.32	.96		.50	.62	.81	.70	.62	.64	.67				.37				
Gov.	1930	e	.19	-.31	.48	.50		.64	.42	.44	.48	.49	.54				.42				-.42
Sen.	1930	f	.66	.16	.47	.62	.64		.68	.65	.61	.59	.52				-.02				-.001
Pres.	1932	g	.55	.03	.68	.81	.42	.68		.95	.82	.83	.77			.32	.17	.32	-.24		
Sen.	1932	h	.58	.17	.55	.70	.44	.65	.95		.82	.83	.77				.12				
Gov.	1934	i	.36	.06	.52	.62	.48	.61	.81	.82		.99	.87	.76			.19	.24			
Sen.	1934	j	.32	.03	.55	.64	.49	.59	.82	.83	.99		.89				.24				
Pres.	1936	k	.26	-.20	.60	.67	.54	.52	.78	.77	.87	.89		.90	.96	.36	.48	.52	-.42		
Sen.	1938	l									.76		.90		.96	.39		.56	-.38		-.35
Pres.	1940	m												.96							
Cath.	1926	n			.76				.32				.36	.39				.34		.36	
Amend. #5	1933	o	-.29	-.66	.48	.37	.42	-.02	.17	.12	.19	.24	.48								-.72
Pro-Repeal	1933	p		-.67	.62				.32		.24		.52	.56		.34			-.73		
Native White	1930	q			-.68				-.24				-.42	-.38				-.73		.54	.67
Vote Shift	1936-1938	r														.36			.54		.58
Rural Farm	1930	s					-.42	-.001						-.35			-.72		.67	.58	

IV: WISCONSIN ELECTION RETURNS: NUMBERS AND PERCENTAGES,
1924-1940

Election	State Totals Votes in Thousands		Per Cent for Candidate (3)	Percentages by Counties			
	Vote for Candidate (1)	Total for Candidates (2)		Mean (4)	Low (5)	High (6)	Sigma (7)
President, 1924		833[1]					
La Follette, Sr. Indep.	454		54.4	55.4	33	71	9.0
Coolidge, Repub.	312		37.4	36.8	19	61	8.6
Davis, Dem.	68		8.2	7.8	2	21	4.0
Governor, 1924		796[2]					
Blaine, Repub.	412		51.8	57.8	31	82	11.3
Senator, 1925		352[2]					
La Follette, Jr. Repub.	238		67.5	70.3	46	85	9.5
Senator, 1926		542[2]					
Blaine, Repub.	301		55.5	58.9	37	86	9.5
President, 1928		1,017[2]					
Hoover, Repub.	544		53.5	57.8	28	76	10.4
Senator, 1928		743[2]					
La Follette, Jr. Repub.	635		85.6	86.3	73	97	5.1
Governor, 1928		989[2]					
Kohler, Repub.	548		55.4	60.1	34	81	10.7
Governor, 1930		606[2]					
La Follette, Repub.	393		63.0	72.4	45	90	10.3
President, 1932		1,055[3]					
Roosevelt, Dem.	707		67.0	65.9	46	86	8.2
Senator, 1932		998[3]					
Duffy, Dem.	610		61.1	59.2	38	77	8.4
Governor, 1932		1,061[3]					
Schmedeman, Dem.	590		55.6	55.9	36	73	7.8
Governor (Primary), 1932		734[3]					
La Follette, Repub.	320		43.6	49.1	25	73	11.1
Senator, 1934		875[1]					
R. La Follette, Jr. Prog.	441		50.4	52.5	33	70	8.7
Callahan, Dem.	223		25.5	22.9	10	42	7.3
Chapple, Repub.	211		24.1	24.7	12	49	7.1
Governor, 1934		906[1]					
P. La Follette, Prog.	373		41.2	44.1	23	63	9.0
Schmedeman, Dem.	359		39.7	35.7	19	57	8.9
Greene, Repub.	173		19.1	20.3	8	39	7.4
President, 1936		1,184[3]					
Roosevelt, Dem.	803		67.8	63.3	44	80	7.9
Governor, 1936		1,206[1]					
P. La Follette, Prog.	574		47.5	48.5	30	67	8.7
Lueck, Dem.	269		22.3	18.5	7	40	8.5
Wiley, Repub.	364		30.2	33.1	22	55	8.0
Senator, 1938		928[1]					
Ekern, Prog.	249		26.8	26.8	11	48	9.4
Duffy, Dem.	232		25.0	22.5	8	44	9.1
Wiley, Repub.	447		48.2	50.7	33	72	8.4

TABLE IV—Continued.

Election	State Totals Votes in Thousands Vote for Candidate (1)	State Totals Votes in Thousands Total for Candidates (2)	Per Cent for Candidate (3)	Percentages by Counties Mean (4)	Percentages by Counties Low (5)	Percentages by Counties High (6)	Percentages by Counties Sigma (7)
Governor, 1938		976[1]					
P. La Follette, Prog.	353		36.2	36.7	17	58	9.8
Bolens, Dem.	87		9.0	7.5	2	18	3.8
Heil, Repub.	535		54.8	55.9	38	75	8.9
President, 1940		1,384[3]					
Roosevelt, Dem.	705		50.9	46.2	26	68	9.6
Senator, 1940		1,336[1]					
R. La Follette, Jr. Prog.	606		45.3	44.2	21	64	9.6
Finnegan, Dem.	177		13.2	11.4	4	27	5.4
Clausen, Repub.	554		41.4	44.6	28	67	8.7
Governor, 1940		1,370[1]					
Loomis, Prog.	546		39.9	39.3	19	67	11.0
McGovern, Dem.	265		19.3	17.1	5	38	8.1
Heil, Repub.	559		40.8	43.8	25	65	8.1

[1]Three parties.
[2]All parties.
[3]Two parties.

V: SELECTED SOCIAL AND ECONOMIC VARIABLES FOR WISCONSIN

Name	Value for State	Mean	Standard Deviation	Range Low	Range High
Per Cent Native White of Total Population, 1930	48.9	51.75	10.21	20	83
Per Cent Rural Farm Population of Total Population, 1930	30.0	45.77	17.57	1	74
Per Cent Roman Catholic, 1926	22.4	21.11		4	53
Per Cent for Repeal, 1926	63.0	56.04	14.84	30	88
Per Cent for Repeal, 1933	82.1	78.23		51	94
Shift in Democratic Presidential Vote:					
1928-1932	+22.7	+24.87		+11	+42
1932-1936	+ .8	— 2.52	6.90	—16	+22
Decrease in Gross Farm Income Per Farm:					
1931-1933	20.5	20.24		5	32
1927-1933	49.6	47.54		19	59
Gross Income Per Farm (Dollars)					
1927	224.2	209.52		71	395
1931	142.3	134.13		53	232
1933	113.1	107.23	37.03	40	220
1936	176.4	165.66	64.38	42	304
Per Cent Receiving Public Assistance, September, 1938	15.5	16.5	10.12	5	56

VI: CORRELATION MATRIX VOTING BEHAVIOR IN WISCONSIN, 1924-1940

	Prog.Dem. Pres.Pres.Gov. 1924 1924 1924	Dem. Rep. Sen. 1925	Rep. Sen. 1926	Rep. Pres.Sen. 1928	Rep. Gov. 1928	Rep. Gov.Pres. 1928	Rep. Dem. Sen. 1930	Dem. Rep. 1932 1932	Prog. Sen. 1932	Dem.Rep. Re- Pres.Gov.peal 1934 1936	Plans of Living 1938	Na- tive White 1929	Rural Farm 1930	Gross Farm In- come 1930	Per Cent Receiving Public Assistance Sept. 1938
Prog. Pres.1924	-.30 -.60	.79	.56 -.14	.58 -.24	.42	.56 .54 -.63	.71	.33	.17 -.30		.38		
Dem. Pres.1924	-.30	.66	-.07 -.35 -.42	.06 -.55 -.56	.28	.32 -.24 -.61	.00		.24 .15		.26		
Dem. Gov. 1924	-.60 .66		-.50 -.67 -.17	.39 -.36 -.72	-.13	-.02 .16 -.69	-.19		.15 .59				
Rep. Sen. 1925	.79 -.07 -.50		.67 -.27	.64 -.28	.31	.58 .54 .57	.51	.41	.29 -.37		.09		
Rep. Sen. 1926	.56 -.35 -.67	.67	-.28	.56 -.01	.47	.46 .36 -.37	.54	.44	.36 -.55		.40		
Rep. Pres. 1928	-.14 -.42 -.17	-.27 -.28		.41 .83	.39	-.72 -.70 .49	.16	-.68	-.83 -.09		.25		
Rep. Sen. 1928	.58 .06 -.39	.64 .56 -.41		-.34	.19	.69 .58 -.60	.34	.41	.40 -.39		.24		
Rep. Gov. 1928	-.24 -.55 -.36	-.28 -.01 .83	-.34		.48	-.64 -.72 .58	.15	-.48	-.66 -.31		.56		
Rep. Gov. 1930	.42 -.56 -.72	.31 .47 .39	.19 .48		-.04	-.13 -.14 .64	-.06		-.47 -.61		-.31		
Dem. Pres. 1932	.56 .28 -.13	.58 .46 -.72	.69 .64 -.04			.91 -.86 .26	.63		.65 -.23	-.03	-.42		
Dem. Sen. 1932	.54 .32 -.02	.54 .36 -.70	.58 -.72 -.13	.91		-.89 .24	.66		.65 -.07		-.54		
Rep. Gov. 1932	-.63 -.24 .16	-.57 -.37 .49	-.60 .58 -.14	-.86 -.89		.39	-.43		-.38 .20		-.04		
Prog. Sen. 1934	.71 -.61 -.69	.51 .54 .16	.34 .15 .64	.26 .24 -.39			.30		-.10 -.30		-.08		
Dem. Pres. 1936	.33 .00 -.19	.41 .44 -.68	.41 -.48 -.06	.63 .66 -.43	.30			-.46	.69 -.04	-.45 -.53 -.17			
Rep. Gov. 1938								-.46		.52 .05 .56 -.68			
Repeal 1929	.17 .24 .15	.29 .36 -.83	.40 -.66 -.47	.65 .65 -.38 -.10		.69			.16		.57		
Plans of Living 1930	-.30 .15 .59	-.37 -.55 -.09	-.39 -.31 -.61	-.23 -.07	.20 -.30	-.04		.16			.07		
Native White 1930						-.03		-.45 .52		.27 .51 -.46			
Rural-Farm 1930	.38 .26		.09 .40 .25	.24 -.56 -.31	-.42	-.54 -.04 -.08	-.53 .05	.57 .07	.27		-.16		
Gross Farm Income 1936								-.17 .56		.51 -.16		-.71	
Percent Rec'g Public Assistance Sept. 1938								-.68		-.46		-.71	

VII: VARIABLES USED IN STUDY OF VOTING BEHAVIOR IN IOWA, 1924-1940

(n = 99)

			Votes Received (in thousands)	Total Vote Cast for State	Percentage for State[1]	Standard Deviation	Percentages by Counties Mean	Lowest	Highest
Pres.	Rep.	1924	537	972	55.3	7.8	54.9	34	69
Sen.	Rep.	1926	323	571	56.6	9.6	58.7	37	87
Pres.	Dem.	1928	379	1,003	37.8	7.8	37.4	23	67
Gov.	Dem.	1930	185	549	33.7	11.7	31.0	12	68
Pres.	Dem.	1932	598	1,012	59.1	6.4	60.0	46	76
Sen.	Dem.	1932	538	982	54.9	7.2	53.9	37	80
Gov.	Dem.	1932	509	964	52.8	8.6	51.5	23	73
Sen.[2]	Rep.	1932	146	343	42.5	12.4	41.5	15	75
Gov.	Dem.	1934	469	864	54.3	7.8	52.6	28	76
Pres.	Dem.	1936	622	1,110	56.0	6.1	55.5	41	69
Sen.	Dem.	1936	540	1,043	51.7	5.4	51.4	39	64
Gov.	Dem.	1936	524	1,046	50.1	5.5	49.8	37	65
Sen.	Dem.	1938	414	825	50.2	7.3	50.0	33	71
Gov.	Dem.	1938	388	835	46.4	5.9	46.6	32	64
Pres.	Dem.	1940	579	1,211	47.8	6.4	46.5	33	59
Gov.	Dem.	1940	554	1,174	47.2	5.8	45.7	33	58

[1]Given only as between two candidates except for President 1924.
[2]Percentages for Brookhart of total Republican primary vote.

VIII: SOCIAL AND ECONOMIC VARIABLES USED IN STUDY OF VOTING BEHAVIOR IN IOWA, 1924-1940

(n = 99)

		Percentage for State	Standard Deviation	Percentages by Counties		
				Mean	Lowest	Highest
Shift—Roosevelt Vote	1932-1936	—3.1	5.0	—4.5	—14	9
Shift—Roosevelt Vote	1936-1940	—8.2	5.4	—9.0	—26	—1
Native White Population of Native Parentage[1]	1930	68.7	12.1	69.4	40	93
Plane of Living	1930		1.5	11.4	8	16
Rural Farm Population	1930	39.0	14.3	48.6	7	70
Repeal Vote	1933	60.2	16.0	55.1	22	94
Newspaper Coverage	1933	37.5	21.1	33.0	1	100
Corn Loss Index	1935-1936	36.4	21.1	41.3	10	97

[1]Total population, 1930, was 2,471,000 and the number of native white population of native parentage, 1930, was 1,698,000.

IX: VARIABLES RELATING TO VOTING BEHAVIOR IN IOWA, 1924-1940
Correlation Matrix, n = 99

		Pres. Rep. 1924 a	Sen. Rep. 1926 b	Pres. Dem. 1928 c	Pres. Dem. 1932 d	Sen. Dem. 1932 e	Gov. Dem. 1932 f	Gov. Dem. 1934 g	Pres. Dem. 1936 h	Sen. Dem. 1936 i	Pres. Dem. 1940 j	Gov. Dem. 1940 k	Rural Farm 1940 l	Native White 1930 m	Repeal Vote 1933 n	News Paper Coverage 1933 o	Shift Roosevelt Vote 1932-1936 p	Net Corn Loss 1935-1936 q
Pres. Rep. 1924	a		—.07	—.78	—.81	—.70	—.56	—.41	—.56	—.57			—.19		—.46	.17		
Sen. Rep. 1926	b	—.07		—.29	.01	—.29	—.41	—.27	.29	.20			.25		—.17	.33		
Pres. Dem. 1928	c	—.78	—.29		.77	.83	.71	.58	.56	.60			.10		.59	—.25		
Pres. Dem. 1932	d	—.81	.01	.77		.81	.66	.50	.68	.70			.30	—.39	.46	—.26	—.44	—.28
Sen. Dem. 1932	e	—.70	—.29	.83	.81		.88	.77	.64	.66			—.08		.77	—.45		
Gov. Dem. 1932	f	—.56	—.41	.71	.66	.88		.80	.47	.52			—.14		.72	—.52		
Gov. Dem. 1934	g	—.41	—.27	.58	.50	.77	.80		.60	.62			—.31		.77	—.45		
Pres. Dem. 1936	h	—.56	.29	.56	.68	.64	.47	.60		.96	.64	.64	—.02	—.62	.55	—.08	.35	.10
Sen. Dem. 1936	i	—.57	.20	.60	.70	.66	.52	.62	.96				.02		.52	—.13		
Pres. Dem. 1940	j								.64			.93						
Gov. Dem. 1940	k								.64		.93							
Rural Farm 1940	l	—.19	.25	.10	.30	—.08	—.14	—.31	—.02	.02				—.03	—.28	.18	—.41	—.15
Native White 1930	m				—.39				—.62				—.03		—.61		—.26	—.23
Repeal Vote 1933	n	—.46	—.17	.59	.46	.77	.72	.77	.55	.52			—.28	—.61		—.58	.08	.25
Newspaper 1933	o	.17	.33	—.25	—.26	—.45	—.52	—.45	—.08	—.13			.18		—.58			
Shift in Vote 1932-1936	p				—.44				.35				—.41	—.26	.08			.49
Net Corn Loss 1936	q				—.28				.10				—.15	—.23	.25		.49	

X: CORRELATION MATRIX, CALIFORNIA ELECTIONS, 1924-1940
(57 counties, omitting Alpine)

			Ret.Pl. Life Paym.Liv. 1938 a	Pl. of Wh. 1930 b	Nat. Farm Pop. 1930 c	Ru- ults Reg. 1930 d	Ad- Re- peal 1930 e	Pro Inc. Tax 1933 f	Pro Anti- Labor 1936 g	Pro Dem. 1938 h	Pres. Rep. 1924 i	Pres. Gov. Dem. 1924 j	Pres. Sen. Dem. 1928 k	Gov. Dem. 1930 l	Pres. Dem. 1932 m	Sen. Dem. 1932 n	Gov. Dem. 1934 o	Pres. Dem. 1936 p	Gov. Dem. 1938 q	Sen. Dem. 1938 r	Sen. Rep. 1932 s	Pres. Dem. 1940 t
Retirement life	1938	a								-.33							.35	.58	.40	.51		
Pl. of Living Native	1930	b		-.57	.05					-.56	.16	-.03	-.06	-.33	-.27	.24	.05				
White Rural-	1930	c		.35						.09			.18	-.05	-.19	-.03	.20					
Farm Adults	1930	d	-.57	.35		.19	-.27			.38	.51	-.22	.07	.43	.37	.34	-.41	-.03	-.14	-.06		
Reg'd	1930	e		-.43	.19	.26				.23	-.14	.07	-.24	.19	-.04	.02	.03					
Pro Repeal	1933	f		.05	-.27	.26				-.02	-.47	.72	.84	.47	.08	.22	.73					
Pro Income Tax	1936	g														.30						
Pro Anti- Lab.	1938	h	-.33		.09	.38								-.36	-.64	-.60	-.71				-.70	
Pres. Dem.	1924	i		-.56	.51	.23	-.02				-.42	.30	.14	.56	.40	-.29	.26					
Pres. Rep.	1924	j		.16	-.22	-.14	-.47			-.42		-.79	.27	-.82	-.61	-.05	-.46					
Pres. Dem.	1928	k		.03	.07	.07	.72			.30	.79		-.52	.80	.53	.03	.76					
Gov. Dem.	1930	l	-.06	.43	-.24	-.84				.14	.27	-.52		-.18	.13	-.27	-.04					
Pres. Dem.	1932	m	-.33	.18	.37	.19	.47			.56	-.82	.80	-.18		.73	.03	.89		.96			
Sen. Dem.	1932	n	-.27		.34	-.04	.08			.40	-.61	.53	.13	.73		-.21	.77	.49		.96		
Gov. Dem.	1934	o	.35	.24	-.05	-.41	.02	.22		.30	-.36	-.29	-.05	.03	-.27	.03	-.21		.12	.33	.39		
Pres. Dem.	1936	p	.58	.05	-.19	-.03	.03	.73		-.64	.26	-.41	.76	-.04	.89	.77	.12		.68	.55		.89	
Gov. Dem.	1938	q	.40		-.03	-.14				-.60						.33	.68		.89				
Sen. Dem.	1938	r	.51		.20	-.06				-.71					.49	.39	.55	.89					
Sen. Rep.	1932	s													.96								
Pres. Dem.	1940	t								-.70						.89							

XI: CALIFORNIA ELECTION RETURNS AND DEMOCRATIC PERCENTAGES

	Votes in Thousands		Per cent Democratic	Democratic Percentages		
	Democratic	Total	Democratic	Mean	Low	High
President 1924						
State excluding three most urban counties	54	538[1]	10			
Los Angeles County	34	457[1]	7			
San Francisco County	10	154[1]	6			
Alameda County	8	132[1]	6			
Total for State	106	1,281[1]	8		6	22
Senator 1926						
State excluding three most urban counties	169	482	35			
Los Angeles County	148	350	42			
San Francisco County	40	114	35			
Alameda County	35	115	31			
Total for State	392	1,061	37		15	47

TABLE XI—Continued.

	Votes in Thousands		Per cent	Democratic Percentages		
	Democratic	Total	Democratic	Mean	Low	High
Governor 1926						
State excluding three most urban counties	138	502	27			
Los Angeles County	64	355	18			
San Francisco County	48	121	40			
Alameda County	32	118	28			
Total for State	282	1,097	26		14	45
President 1928						
State excluding three most urban counties	429	247	37			
Los Angeles County	508	210	29			
San Francisco County	94	96	51			
Alameda County	117	61	34			
Total for State	1,148	614	35	40.2	20	56
Senator 1928						
State excluding three most urban counties	107	551	20			
Los Angeles County	121	593	21			
San Francisco County	26	139	19			
Alameda County	28	149	19			
Total for State	282	1,431	20		11	27
Governor 1930						
State excluding three most urban counties	135	597	23			
Los Angeles County	165	464	36			
San Francisco County	15	145	10			
Alameda County	19	127	15			
Total for State	334	1,333	25	21.3	10	44
President 1932						
State excluding three most urban counties	520	834	62			
Los Angeles County	554	928	60			
San Francisco County	144	214	67			
Alameda County	106	196	54			
Total for State	1,324	2,172	61	66.3	48	78
Senator 1932						
State excluding three most urban counties	383	839	46			
Los Angeles County	418	948	44			
San Francisco County	62	191	32			
Alameda County	80	195	41			
Total for State	943	2,173	43	47.5	32	65

TABLE XI—Continued.

| | Votes in Thousands | | Per cent | Democratic Percentages | | |
	Democratic	Total	Democratic	Mean	Low	High
Governor 1934						
State excluding three most						
urban counties	313	942	33			
Los Angeles County	405	961	42			
San Francisco County	88	224	39			
Alameda County	73	193	38			
Total for State	879	2,320	38	33.2	19	46
Senator 1934						
State excluding three most						
urban counties	805	847	95			
Los Angeles County	804	845	95			
San Francisco County	174	188	93			
Alameda County	164	175	94			
Total for State	1,947	2,055	95		92	97
President 1936						
State excluding three most						
urban counties	664	995	67			
Los Angeles County	757	1,115	68			
San Francisco County	196	261	75			
Alameda County	149	232	64			
Total for State	1,766	2,603	68	68.1	50	80
Governor 1938						
State excluding three most						
urban counties	538	1,045	52			
Los Angeles County	612	1,059	58			
San Francisco County	132	243	54			
Alameda County	109	216	51			
Total for State	1,391	2,563	54	51.0	39	63
President 1940						
State excluding three most						
urban counties	721	1,259	57			
Los Angeles County	823	1,397	59			
San Francisco County	186	308	60			
Alameda County	148	265	56			
Total for State	1,878	3,229	58	58.9	33	73

[1]Includes Progressive vote.

XII: POLITICAL VARIABLES: ILLINOIS COOK COUNTY AND DOWNSTATE

| | Cook County and Downstate | | | Democratic Percentages | | | |
| | Votes in Thousands | | Per Cent | By Counties | | | |
	Democratic	Total	Democratic	Mean	Sigma	Lowest	Highest
President 1924							
Cook County	226	1,111	20	----	----	----	----
Rest of State	351	1,351	27	30.2	13.79	----	----
Total	577	2,462	24	----	----	5	58
Governor 1924							
Cook County	447	1,081	41	----	----	----	----
Rest of State	574	1,307	44	45.6	9.35	----	----
Total	1,021	2,388	43	----	----	23	74
President 1928							
Cook County	716	1,528	47	----	----	----	----
Rest of State	598	1,555	38	38.5	9.39	----	----
Total	1,314	3,083	43	----	----	19	69
Governor 1928							
Cook County	655	1,481	44	----	----	----	----
Rest of State	630	1,514	42	42.0	9.37	----	----
Total	1,285	2,995	43	----	----	17	65
Representatives-at-Large 1928							
Cook County	1,215	2,808	43	----	----	----	----
Rest of State	1,067	2,860	37	38.0	10.07	----	----
Total	2,282	5,668	40	----	----	15	67
Representatives-at-Large 1930							
Cook County	1,144	1,957	58	----	----	----	----
Rest of State	894	1,962	46	44.8	11.19	----	----
Total	2,038	3,919	52	----	----	17	70
President 1932							
Cook County	919	1,609	57	----	----	----	----
Rest of State	963	1,706	56	57.5	8.22	----	----
Total	1,882	3,315	57	----	----	30	75
Governor 1932							
Cook County	1,034	1,617	64	----	----	----	----
Rest of State	896	1,677	54	53.4	7.52	----	----
Total	1,930	3,294	59	----	----	32	70
Representatives-at-Large 1932							
Cook County	1,676	3,031	55	----	----	----	----
Rest of State	1,655	3,128	53	53.4	7.52	----	----
Total	3,331	6,159	54	----	----	25	71

TABLE XII—Continued.

| | Cook County and Downstate Votes in Thousands | | Per Cent | Democratic Percentages By Counties | | | |
	Democratic	Total	Democratic	Mean	Sigma	Lowest	Highest
Representatives - at-Large 1934							
Cook County	1,617	2,588	63				
Rest of State	1,351	2,694	50	49.7	7.11		
Total	2,968	5,282	56			28	66
President 1936							
Cook County	1,253	1,954	64				
Rest of State	1,030	1,897	54	57.8	7.33		
Total	2,283	3,851	59			31	74
Governor 1936							
Cook County	1,087	1,882	58				
Rest of State	981	1,869	53	51.6	6.82		
Total	2,068	3,751	55			31	65
Representatives - at-Large 1936							
Cook County	2,230	3,680	61				
Rest of State	1,865	3,549	53	51.5	7.36		
Total	4,095	7,229	57			30	66
Representatives - at-Large 1938							
Cook County	1,802	3,156	57				
Rest of State	1,331	2,906	46	46.5	8.60		
Total	3,133	6,062	52			25	65
President 1940							
Cook County	1,168	2,107	55				
Rest of State	982	2,091	47	45.0	7.67		
Total	2,150	4,198	51			27	60
Governor 1940							
Cook County	1,015	2,092	49				
Rest of State	926	2,047	45	44.5	7.47		
Total	1,941	4,139	47			25	58
Representatives - at-Large 1940							
Cook County	2,122	4,038	53				
Rest of State	1,760	3,915	45	44.0	7.81		
Total	3,882	7,953	49			25	58

XIII: INTERCORRELATIONS OF VARIABLES RELATING TO VOTING BEHAVIOR IN ILLINOIS, 1924-1938
(101 Downstate Counties)

Letter Symbol	Pro-Repeal 1930 a	Native White 1930 b	Rural Farm 1930 c	Catholic 1926 d	Republican President 1924 e	Democrat Pres. 1924 f	Progressive Pres. 1924 g	Democrat for Gov-'nor 1928 h	Democrat for President 1928 i	Democrat for Cong. man at large 1930 j	Democrat for Gov-'nor 1932 k	Democrat for President 1932 l	Democrat for Gov-'nor 1936 m	Democrat for President 1936 n	Democrat for Congress-men at large 1938 o	Relative Relief Burdens 1938-39 p
Pro-Repeal	a	1.00	-.74	-.61	.67	.11	-.52	.63	.03	.22	-.02	.01	-.04	-.03	.08	-.18	-.08
Nat. White	b	-.74	1.00	.60	-.55	-.48	.82	-.65	.31	.17	.45	.35	.43	.37	.25	.55	.28
Rural-Farm	c	-.61	.60	1.00	-.22	-.17	.52	-.58	.08	.03	.11	.05	.19	-.09	-.18	.14	-.06
Catholic	d	.67	-.55	-.22	1.00	-.12	-.30	.59	.23	.44	.15	.13	.17	.00	.08	-.04	-.23
Rep.Pres. 1924	e	.11	-.48	-.17	-.17	1.00	-.74	-.07	-.86	-.82	-.89	-.78	-.87	-.74	-.71	-.89	-.44
Dem.Pres. 1924	f	-.52	.82	.52	-.30	-.74	1.00	-.62	.62	.52	.73	.66	.68	.60	.50	.80	.40
Prog.Pres. 1924	g	.63	-.65	-.58	.59	-.07	-.62	1.00	.08	.19	-.05	-.08	.01	-.03	.09	-.16	-.07
Gov. 1928	h	.03	.31	.08	.23	-.86	.62	.08	1.00	.87	.91	.79	.90	.77	.76	.84	.34
Pres.1928	i	.22	.17	.03	.44	-.82	.52	.19	.87	1.00	.84	.72	.84	.63	.66	.73	.33
Cong.1930	j	-.02	.45	.11	.15	-.89	.73	-.05	.91	.84	1.00	.87	.90	.77	.75	.87	.34
Gov.1932	k	.01	.35	.05	.13	-.78	.66	-.08	.79	.72	.87	1.00	.82	.74	.72	.80	.26
Pres.1932	l	-.04	.43	.19	.17	-.87	.68	.01	.90	.84	.90	.82	1.00	.81	.80	.86	.29
Gov. 1936	m	-.03	.37	-.09	.00	-.74	.60	-.03	.77	.63	.77	.74	.81	1.00	.96	.87	.34
Pres.1936	n	.08	.25	-.18	.08	-.71	.50	.09	.76	.66	.75	.72	.80	.96	1.00	.83	.32
Cong.1938	o	-.18	.55	.14	-.04	-.89	.80	-.16	.84	.73	.87	.80	.86	.87	.83	1.00	.52
Relief	p	-.08	.28	-.06	-.23	-.44	.40	-.07	.34	.33	.34	.26	.29	.34	.32	.52	1.00

XIV: LOUISIANA PRIMARY ELECTION RETURNS AND PRO-LONG CANDIDATES PERCENTAGES, 1924-1940

Democratic Primaries, 1924-1940	Votes in Thousands			Per cent for State for Pro-Long Candidates	Percentages by Counties for Pro-Long Candidates			Per Cent for Orleans County for Pro-Long Candidates	Per Cent for Balance of State for Pro-Long Candidates
	Pro-Long Candidates[1]	Anti-Long Candidates	Total		Mean	Low	High		
Governor, 1924- 1st	74	166	240	30.9	37.0	3.0	76.4	17.7	36.2
Governor, 1924- 2nd	92	126	218	42.2	42.2	5.1	85.0	39.0	43.6
Senator, 1924	104	86	190	54.9	50.9	19.8	94.9	67.0	50.0
Senator, 1926	84	81	165	51.0	48.1	11.4	85.5	52.2	50.4
Governor, 1928	127	162	289	43.9	52.0	15.9	73.6	22.7	51.8
Senator, 1930	150	111	261	57.3	62.4	17.2	99.8	47.1	62.0
Governor, 1932	215	165	380	56.5	54.1	34.6	100.0	70.7	51.5
Senator, 1932	181	125	306	59.2	58.0	34.1	99.5	64.7	57.0
Governor, 1936	363	177	540	67.1	66.1	46.2	98.2	72.0	65.3
Senator, 1936	365	172	537	68.0	67.4	47.2	98.2	72.3	66.4
Senator, 1936 (unexpired term)	368	168	536	68.7	68.5	47.9	98.4	72.2	67.5
Governor, 1940- 1st	226	328	554	40.9	39.8	23.0	67.0	50.0	37.7
Governor, 1940- 2nd	264	283	547	48.2	47.9	32.9	80.7	55.3	45.7

[1]See Footnote 30 on p. 185.

REFERENCES

Chapter I

1. H. F. Gosnell, ''The Improvement of Present Public Opinion Analysis,'' in Douglas Waples (ed.), *Print, Radio and Film in a Democracy* (Chicago, 1942), pp. 118-132; A. B. Blankenship, ''The Effect of the Interviewer Upon the Response in a Public Opinion Poll,'' *Journal of Consulting Psychology*, IV (1940); Daniel Katz, ''Do Interviewers Bias the Polls?'' *Public Opinion Quarterly*, VI (Summer, 1942), pp. 248-68.

2. Daniel Katz, ''The Public Opinion Polls and the 1940 Election,'' *Public Opinion Quarterly*, V (March, 1941), pp. 52-78.

3. H. F. Gosnell, ''The Negro Vote in Northern Cities,'' *National Municipal Review*, XXX (May, 1941), 264-67; Edward H. Litchfield, ''A Case Study of Negro Political Behavior in Detroit,'' *Public Opinion Quarterly*, V (June, 1941), pp. 267-74.

4. George Gallup and Saul Forbes Rae, *The Pulse of Democracy; The Public Opinion Poll and How It Works* (New York, 1940) pp. 162-63.

CHAPTER II

1. There is a growing body of literature on this subject, but the possibilities have hardly been tapped. See F. Y. Edgeworth, "Miscellaneous Applications of the Calculus of Probabilities," *Journal of the Royal Statistical Society*, LXI (September, 1898), pp. 534-44, in which he studies the swing of the pendulum in three British parliamentary elections; S. A. Rice, "Time Series: Party Turnover in New Jersey, 1877-1924," in his *Quantitative Methods in Politics* (New York, 1928), chap. xxi; W. B. Munro, "The Law of the Pendulum" in his *The Invisible Government* (New York, 1928); P. S. Florence, *The Statistical;* A. M. Schlesinger, "Tides of American Politics," *Yale Review*, XXXIX (December, 1939), pp. 217-30.

2. Courtesy of Mr. Louis Bean of the United States Department of Agriculture. See his *Ballot Behavior: A Study of Presidential Elections* (Washington, D. C., 1940).

3. See "Disintegration of the Democratic Party," *New Republic* XLIX (February 9, 1927), pp. 316-18; "Why Should the Democratic Party Survive?" *Nation*, CXIX (November 19, 1924), pp. 534-35.

4. Bean points out that from 1854 to 1940 the amplitude of the national swings has varied from sixteen to twenty-four years. (*Op. cit.*, chap. VII.). See also A. M. Schlesinger, *op. cit.*

5. A. N. Holcombe's *The Political Parties of Today* (New York, 1924) is outstanding, but the book has not been brought to date. For the later period see R. V. Peel and T. C. Donnelly, *The 1928 Campaign* (New York, 1931) and their *The 1932 Campaign* (New York, 1935).

6. This type of approach is found in A. W. Macmahon, "Political Parties— United States," *Encyclopaedia of the Social Sciences*, XI (1933), pp. 596-601, and in V. B. Boothe, *The Political Party as a Social Process* (Philadelphia, 1923).

7. For a discussion of some of the early studies see H. F. Gosnell, "Statisticians and Political Scientists," *American Political Science Review*, XXVII (June, 1933), pp. 399-400. Bean, *op. cit.*, chap. VIII, has handled the problem better than some of the earlier writers, but he runs into difficulties because he ignores the relationship between party control of the presidency and party control of Congress. For 1920 he has a negative business index and a positive index for percentage change of major party. This is correct if Congress only is considered. But in 1920 the Democrats controlled the presidency and an increase in the Republican vote should give a negative index for the change in the major party. The reference dates used for the analysis of the relations between business and political cycles in the text are taken from Wesley C. Mitchell, "Business Cycles," *Encyclopaedia of the Social Sciences*, III (1930), p. 95.

8. This subject has not been adequately treated. Concerning the 1916 and 1920 elections, see Holcombe, *op. cit.* In 1940 the gains made by Roosevelt in the coastal states clearly indicate the importance of national defense to these areas. The most isolationist states were in the middle west.

9. Bean (*op. cit.*) presents other charts which are of considerable interest.

10. Those who are not familiar with statistical methods should read Appendix I first. In the notes that follow, such elementary knowledge of quantitative techniques as is outlined there will be assumed. Bean, *op. cit.*, presents a graphic solution of the problems involved.

11. This grouping is based upon an examination of the difference between the national and state means, the state standard deviation, the regression equation between the state and the nation, and the standard error of estimate.

12. If a state percentage were exactly the same as the national percentage, then the slope, b, of the regression line would be 1 and the constant, a, would be 0. By parallel is meant that the regression line is parallel to the 45 degree angle line. As b approaches 1 we may say that the state comes closer to paralleling national trends. In the case of Ohio we find the following situation:

Let X_1 = the percentage of the combined Republican and Democratic vote that was Democratic for Ohio in the presidential elections from 1896 to 1940 omitting 1912. Let X_2 = the percentage of the combined Republican and Democratic vote that was Democratic for the nation as a whole in the presidential elections from 1896 to 1940, omitting 1912.

Then X_1 = $-0.16 + .96X_2$; S_{12} = 3.65; σ_1 = 9.0; σ_2 = 8.6; M_1 = 45.5; M_2 = 47.3; Md_1 = 47; Md_2 = 47; range for X_1, 61-29 = 32; range for X_2, 62-35 = 27.

A comparison of the values of the a and b constants for this equation with all the others given below shows that Ohio comes nearest to fulfilling the ideal conditions. Since the number of cases is very small (n = 11) and since the distributions are not normal in all cases, the use of correlational techniques is doubtful. If unlimited funds were available it would be preferable to present the time series and the scatter diagrams by themselves. The correlational techniques are used merely as a short cut method of presenting the data.

13. $M_2 - M_1$ = 1.8.

14. For purposes of convenience, the means, standard deviations, ranges, coefficients of correlation, and regression equations for the states which parallel national trends during the period 1896-1940 omitting 1912 are presented below. The value of the b constant in the regression equation does not fall below .85 or exceed 1.15. This classification is arbitrary, but convenient.

STATES WHICH PARALLEL NATIONAL TRENDS

Characteristics of States with Republican Bias

State	M	Md	σ	High	Low	Range (4) minus (5)	r	Regression Constants a	b	S Mean Deviation between state and nation
Mass.	41.8	40	10.0	55	27	28	.74	.59	.87	6.69	5.5
Vt.	29.2	23	10.4	45	17	28	.81	—17.1	.98	6.11	18.1
N. J.	42.7	41	8.5	60	30	30	.94	— 1.6	.94	2.78	4.6
N. Y.	45.5	45	8.8	60	29	31	.88	2.9	.90	4.16	1.8
Pa.	38.8	37	10.1	58	23	35	.96	—14.8	1.13	2.83	8.5
Kans.	42.3	45	10.6	55	27	28	.85	— 7.1	1.04	5.65	5.0
Ill.	43.2	43	9.9	59	27	32	.96	— 9.6	1.12	2.79	4.1

With Democratic Bias.

State	M	Md	σ	High	Low	Range (4) minus (5)	r	Regression Constants a 5	b 4	S Mean Deviation between state and nation
[1]Okla.	56.0	56	10.7	73	36	37	.80	13.3	.89	6.46	—7.7
[2]Colo.	48.3	50	11.6	64	28	36	.84	— 2.7	1.08	6.36	—1.0
[3]Utah	50.1	47	11.3	70	35	35	.91	— 4.1	1.15	4.61	—2.8
Ariz.	57.0	62	11.7	72	42	30	.97	3.6	1.10	2.98	—8.4
Neb.	46.3	48	11.1	64	27	37	.80	— 2.9	1.04	6.60	1.0

[1] = % Dem. Pres. U. S. 1900-1940, omitting 1912.
[2] = % Dem. Pres. U. S. 1916-1940.
[3] = % Dem. Pres. U. S. 1908-1940, omitting 1912.

In general the difference between a Republican and a Democratic bias or basic tendency is determined by M. If the M for the state is higher than for the nation as a whole, then the state has a Democratic bias, if lower a Republican bias. However, where the median and the mean (M) are not the same, the median is followed. There are a number of cases where it is very difficult to determine whether a state had a Republican or a Democratic bias during the period under discussion. A third classification might have been introduced, namely, the doubtful states, but this would have complicated the presentation of the materials.

15. See note 20 below.

16. Theodore Roosevelt and Alton B. Parker were both natives of New York; Cox and Harding were natives of Ohio. In 1940 F. D. Roosevelt and Wendell Willkie were residents of New York, but Willkie made much of the fact that he was born in Indiana.

17. All states whose b constant in the regression equation of state on na-

tion is more than 1.15. This is an arbitrary line. Iowa closely resembles Nebraska, given above as a parallel state.

18. The relationships of the states with greater swing (flexibility) and Republican bias during the period 1896-1940 (omitting 1912) are:

State	M	Md	σ	High	Low	Range (4) minus (5)	r	Regression Constants a	b	S	Mean Deviation between state and nation
Mich.	38.4	40	13.2	59	15	44	.98	—32.9	1.51	2.87	8.9
Wis.	41.8	40	15.6	68	18	50	.94	—39.1	1.71	5.28	5.5
Minn.	40.1	41	16.5	67	12	55	.96	—46.9	1.84	4.84	7.2
S. D.	40.8	42	13.3	65	21	44	.90	—24.9	1.39	5.85	6.5
N. D.	40.9	44	17.9	71	13	58	.92	—50.4	1.93	6.91	6.4
Wyo.	44.3	42	12.1	62	24	38	.95	—19.1	1.34	3.82	3.0
Iowa	41.2	42	10.6	59	23	36	.96	—15.3	1.20	2.78	6.1
Wash.	43.4	44	17.1	69	16	53	.95	—45.7	1.88	5.54	3.9
Ore.	44.2	42	12.9	68	22	46	.92	—21.0	1.38	5.15	3.1
Cal.	42.5	43	15.5	68	13	55	.98	—41.0	1.77	3.44	4.8

19. The relationships of the states with greater swing and Democratic bias during the period 1896-1940 (omitting 1912) are:

State	M	Md	σ	High	Low	Range (4) minus (5)	r	Regression Constants a	b	S	Mean Deviation between state and nation
¹Mont.	50.4	53.5	13.2	72	31	41	.96	—16.3	1.41	3.60	—3.1
¹Idaho	45.3	46.5	13.5	65	26	39	.96	—22.5	1.43	3.92	2.0
¹Nev.	52.7	55.0	13.2	73	34	39	.96	—13.8	1.41	3.79	—5.4

[1] = % Dem. Pres. U. S. 1900-1940, omitting 1912.

20. All states whose b constant in the regression equation state on nation is less than .85. This is an arbitrary method of classification. The difference between Massachusetts, in the parallel class above, and Maine is not great.

21. Because Maine holds its congressional elections in September in presidential years, it has acquired a reputation of being something of a political barometer. Claude Robinson has challenged this view in his book *Straw Polls*. Maine is not the best political barometer in the United States but when allowance is made for its Republican bias and for its traditionalism, it may be used as a very rough guide to national trends. Of course, the saying "as Maine goes, so goes the nation" should not be taken literally. In the period

from 1896 to 1940, Maine went Democratic only once—in 1912, when the Republican party was split. Nevertheless, there is some relationship between the Maine votes and the national votes. The pattern is not neat and sharp, but it is discernible. In 1940 the state moved in a direction contrary to the trend it had displayed in the period 1900-1936. With a decline in the national Democratic vote, one would have expected a decline in Maine's vote for Roosevelt, but the opposite happened. In this, Maine was typical of New England. The national defense issue improved Roosevelt's position greatly in this area in 1940.

22. States with less swing and Democratic bias are Maryland, Indiana, Missouri, and New Mexico.

23. Its standard error of estimate (S) is lowest.

24. As shown by scatter diagrams. The statistical characteristics of the distributions were not calculated.

CHAPTER III

1. See Chapter II, above.

2. See Chapter II, note 14.

3. Pennsylvania State Planning Board, *Preliminary Report* (Harrisburg, 1934), p. 419.

4. *Ibid.*, p. 236.

5. The eastern industrial and mining region composed of the anthracite fields and corollary industrial areas including Lackawanna (containing Scranton with a population of 143,000), Northampton (Bethlehem with 60,000), Lehigh (Allentown with 92,500), Dauphin (Harrisburg with 80,000), Luzerne (Wilkes-Barre with 86,500), Schuylkill, Carbon and parts of Berks (Reading with 111,000), Northumberland and Lebanon counties.

6. The western industrial and mining region containing Allegheny (Pittsburgh with 670,000), Beaver, Armstrong, Somerset, Fayette, Cambria (Johnstown with 70,000), Blair, Clearfield, Clarion, Jefferson, Indiana, Butler, Westmoreland, Washington, and parts of Mercer and Lawrence counties.

7. *Fifteenth Census of the United States*, 1930, Agriculture, Vol I, p. 526.

8. The foremost agricultural counties in the order of importance are: value of livestock, Lancaster, Chester, York, Berks, Bradford; value of field and fruit crops, Lancaster, York, Berks, Franklin, Chester; value of milk, eggs, wool and honey, Lancaster, Chester, Bradford, Susquehanna and Crawford. *Ninth Industrial Directory of the Commonwealth of Pennsylvania* (Department of Internal Affairs, Harrisburg, 1938), pp. 10-11. In Lancaster County 30.5 per cent of the farms are operated by tenants but only 3.3 per cent in Sullivan County. Many townships in the eastern areas, according to the 1930 census, have an average value per acre of more than $150. On the other hand the land values in the

northern, central and south-central counties are extremely low. Pennsylvania State Planning Board, *op. cit.*, p. 87.

9. Walter Davenport, *Power and Glory: The Life of Boies Penrose* (New York: G. P. Putnam's Sons, 1931), pp. 94-95.

10. From the records of the Pennsylvania Department of Internal Affairs, furnished by the Pennsylvania State Planning Board.

11. Pennsylvania Department of Agriculture, *Crop and Livestock Report*, 1929, 1938; *Agricultural Statistics*, 1930-1931; *Pennsylvania Crop and Livestock* Report, 1932, 1933, 1934, 1935, 1936, and 1937; *passim*.

12. Two counties, Cameron and Blair, were eliminated from all analyses involving the index number, due to the fact that abnormal shifts of industrial establishments there made the index numbers meaningless.

13. The mean shift in index numbers for the 65 counties, 1928-1932, was —46.89.

14. Pennsylvania Department of Labor and Industry, *How Many are Job-less in Pennsylvania?* (Special Bulletin No. 13, July, 1931), p. 7.

15. *Ibid.*

16. *Ibid.*

17. Pennsylvania Department of Agriculture, *Pennsylvania Crop and Livestock Report*, 1928 and 1933, *passim*.

18. A coefficient of correlation of —.231 results from such a comparison.

19. If the variables of rural-farm population and native-white population are held constant by means of the technique of partial correlation, a much higher coefficient, —.47, is obtained. For figures, see H. F. Gosnell and W. G. Colman, "Political Trends in Industrial America: Pennsylvania an Example," *Public Opinion Quarterly*, IV (September, 1940), p. 477.

20. Walter Davenport, "Pennsylvania—Of All Places," *Colliers*, Vol. 95, (March 23, 1935), pp. 10-11.

21. Gosnell and Colman, *op. cit.*, p. 479.

22. The 12 highest counties are: Fayette (69 per cent for Roosevelt), Washington (69), Allegheny (68), Berks (68), Westmoreland (67), Cambria (66), Beaver (65), Greene (65), Elk (62), Northampton (62), Philadelphia (62), Lackawanna (61).

23. See Chapter V, below.

24. These results were obtained by tabulating percentage for Roosevelt by cities of different population classes.

25. *Pittsburgh Press*, November 4, 1936, p. 14; *Philadelphia Evening Bulletin*, October 31, 1936, p. 1; *Philadelphia Evening Public Ledger*, November 4, 1936, p. 26; *Philadelphia Inquirer*, November 5, 1936, p. 13.

26. *New York Times*, April 28, 1938, p. 1.

27. *Ibid.*, February 18, 1938, p. 8.

28. X_a = per cent vote for Jones for Governor. X_b = per cent vote for Earle for Senator. $M_a = 42.269$; $M_b = 40.239$.

29. This is shown by a tabulation percentage for Roosevelt by mining areas.

30. X_q = vote for Earle for Senator, 1938

X_j = per cent of population on WPA, 1938

$$r_{qj} = .291 \qquad M_q = 40.2388 \qquad \sigma_q = 7.0332$$
$$M_j = 10.2537 \qquad \sigma_j = 4.3959$$
$$X_q = 35.46 + .47X_j \qquad S_{qj} = 6.73$$

Relief figures are from the records of the Pennsylvania State Department of Public Assistance and the Works Progress Administration of Pennsylvania and as presented in David Scheinman, *The Division of the Costs of Unemployment Relief in Massachusetts, Illinois, and Pennsylvania.*

31. Jay G. Hayden in the *Philadelphia Evening Bulletin*, October 3, 1936, p. 1; *Pittsburgh Press*, October 31, 1936, p. 27, and November 4, 1936, p. 14.

32. Pennsylvania Department of Public Instruction, *Pennsylvania—An Inventory of the Human and Economic Resources of the Commonwealth* (Harrisburg, 1936, p. 73.

33. *Fifteenth Census of the United States*, 1930, Vol. III, Part 2, p. 670.

34. *Religious Bodies:* 1926 (United States Bureau of the Census, 1930), Vol. I, pp. 241-47. The existing data on religious affiliation by county leaves much to be desired. Preliminary reports on the 1936 Religious Census are only now being released.

35. *Fifteenth Census of the United States*, pp. 676-79.

36. *Ibid.*, pp. 680-84.

37. From figures supplied through the courtesy of the Secretary of the Commonwealth, Harrisburg, Pennsylvania.

38. The counties exhibiting the above characteristics to the most marked degree are Lackawanna (Wyoming Valley anthracite region); Allegheny (western Pennsylvania industrial and mining region); Schuylkill (southern anthracite fields); Carbon (southern anthracite fields); Cambria (Allegheny Mountains coal mining region); Elk (Upper Allegheny oil and gas region); Westmoreland (western Pennsylvania industrial and mining region); Philadelphia (Philadelphia urban district); and Erie (Erie urban and fruit region). See classification of economic geographic regions, *Preliminary Report of the Pennsylvania State Planning Board*, 1934, p. 278.

39. Gosnell and Colman, *op. cit.*, p. 481.

40. *Ibid.*

41. *Ibid.*

42. A coefficient of —.33 from a comparison of the vote for Earle for governor in 1934 and rural-farm population indicates a beginning of this trend:

X_m = Earle, 1934 $\qquad M_m = 49.9 \qquad \sigma_m = 8.0913 \qquad S_{mc} = 7.6$

The 1934 Earle vote bore slight relationship to the other variables, as was discerned from inspection of the scatter diagrams.

43. *Ibid.*

44. *Ibid.*

It must be pointed out, however, that the zero-order coefficients give no idea of the relative importance of the various independent social variables in relation to the particular political variable. In order to afford such an idea it is necessary to express the vote as a function of the different variables. This will be done in a later part of the study by the standard technique of net regression.

45. Of the fifteen counties returning the highest percentage vote for Earle in 1938, all but one (Greene, a traditionally Democratic county) definitely belonged to the industrial and mining group.

46. The minimum Democratic mean percentage was 25, the minimum Republican mean percentage 48. The sum of these two is 73.

47. Let X_a = vote for Guffey for Senator, 1934 (per cent)

X_b = vote for Roosevelt, 1932 (per cent)

X_c = vote for Pinchot in Republican primary (per cent)

$$X_a = 18.1144 + .7670\ X_b - .0532\ X_c$$

$$S_{a \cdot bc} = 4.80 \qquad R_{a \cdot bc} = .818 \qquad r_{ab} = .816$$

The above equation clearly shows that the vote for Pinchot in the primary—in which he was opposed by David A. Reed, Old Guard reactionary—practically is ineffective in explaining the vote for Guffey in the general election. The coefficient of multiple correlation is practically the same as the zero-order for Guffey and Roosevelt.

Inspection of scatter diagrams of the Pinchot primary vote in 1938 (Pinchot vs. James) with the Earle vote in the general election, 1938, indicates no noticeable relationship of Pinchot with Earle in that year. See also Isadore Feinstein, ''Gentleman in Politics,'' *American Mercury*, May, 1933.

48. The Roosevelt vote as a function of the Smith vote is expressed by the following equation:

X_a = Roosevelt, 1932 $M_a = 45.7$ $\sigma_a = 9.0471$

X_b = Smith, 1928 $M_b = 27.1$ $\sigma_b = 10.6055$

$X_a = 29.96 + .58\ X_b$ $S_{ba} = 6.63$ $r_{ba} = .68$

Note the rather low *b* value and the large S. In the Chicago study the corresponding r was .94. See H. F. Gosnell, *Machine Politics* (Chicago, 1937), p. 109.

49. Gosnell and Colman, *op. cit.*, 484.

50. However, the regression equation (X_e = Earle, 1938 and X_d = Roosevelt 1936) is $X_e = 5.18 + .67\ X_d$. $S_{ed} = 3.07$. The lower *b* value than that found in a comparison of the 1936 and 1934 elections indicates a weakening of New Deal traditional vote in 1938 although the *a* and *S* values remain small.

51. X_f = Roosevelt, 1940 $M_f = 46.7$ $\sigma_f = 9.52$

$X_f = -3.69 + .97\ X_d$ $r_{fd} = .96$

52. Gosnell and Colman, *op. cit.*, 484.

53. $X_g = $ Guffy, 1940 $M_g = 45.6$ $\sigma_g = 9.34$

   $X_t = .43 + 1.016X_g$ $r_{tg} = .996$

54. See Chapters IV-VII, below.

55. Thus the 1938 Earle percentage in each county may be said to consist of a constant, 3, plus 71 per cent of Roosevelt's 1936 vote, less 7 per cent of the native-white percentage, plus 13 per cent of the rural-farm percentage, plus 17 per cent of the WPA percentage. For the 67 counties of the state, this formula will give the closest approximation to the 1938 vote of any possible formula using these variables.

CHAPTER IV

1. See Chapter II, above.

2. See Charles O. Paullin, *Atlas of Historical Geography of the United States* (Washington, D. C., 1932).

3. L. H. Look, ''Ruling Dynasty of Wisfollette,'' *Saturday Evening Post*, CCIII, (1930), pp. 18-19.

4. Up to 1930, the Wisconsin state legislature was overwhelmingly Republican (both stalwart and progressive varieties). Of one hundred members of the House of Representatives, from eighty-three to ninety-two were Republicans in the years 1924-30, and only one or two were Democrats. In 1930, there was a slight foreshadowing of the coming Democratic landslide. The Republicans lost nineteen men in the House, principally to an independent Republican group. In the House, the Republicans dropped from a majority of sixty-four to a minority of thirty-six, while the Democrats increased from two to sixty. With the launching of the new Progressive party by the La Follettes in 1934, came an acceleration in the anti-Republican trend. The La Follette party gained forty-four seats at the expense of the seemingly moribund G. O. P. and the newly resurrected Democrats. The Republicans were left with only eighteen seats—a loss of sixty-seven in six years. In 1936 the Republicans made gains in both houses of the state legislature. In 1938 the regular Republicans gained thirty-three more seats in the House, drawing about equally from Progressive and Democratic sources. Wisconsin appeared to have travelled the whole cycle by 1938 and to be in almost the same political condition as in 1930, except that her Republicanism was of a more conservative tinge.

5. See Table IV, Appendix II.

6. The southeastern section, centering around Milwaukee, and the Lake Shore-Winnebago area centering around Lake Michigan and Lake Winnebago.

7. Average of prices, January 1910 to December 1914 = 100. See Wisconsin Department of Agriculture and Markets, *Wisconsin Crop and Livestock Reporter*, XVIII (July, 1939), p. 44.

8. Wisconsin Department of Agriculture, *Wisconsin Crop and Livestock Reporting Service*, Bulletin No. 188, pp. 1-3, 31.

9. Let X_a = the percentage of the total vote for Roosevelt in 1932 by counties

   Let X_b = the gross farm income per farm in 1933 by counties

   Then r_{ab} = —.07.

10. Let X_c = decrease in gross farm income 1931-1933

    Let X_d = percentage for Roosevelt in 1932 less the percentage for Smith in 1928

    Then r_{cd} = .35.

11. The following sectional division is taken from the *First Annual Report of the Wisconsin Regional Planning Commission*, map 7, p. 207, with modifications based upon the *Wisconsin Agriculture Bulletins*.

12. The northeastern area consists of the counties of Forest, Florence, Marinette, Langlade, and Oconto; the northwestern section contains Douglas, Bayfield, Burnett, Washburn, Sawyer, and Rusk counties.

13. T. Kirkpatrick and A. M. Boyton, *Wisconsin's Human and Physical Resources* (Madison, Wisconsin, 1936), pp. 1-20, 130-40.

14. We have taken Jackson, Juneau, and Adams counties as the poor central sands area.

15. Prairie section is made up of Green, Rock, Walworth, Dane, Jefferson, Columbia, Dodge, and Green Lake counties. The southwestern area consists of La Fayette, Grant, Iowa, Crawford, Richland, Vernon, and Sauk counties.

16. The southeastern counties are Milwaukee, Racine, Kenosha, and Waukesha. The Lake Winnebago and Michigan-Lake Shore counties are: Door, Kewaunee, Brown, Outagamie, Waupaca, Winnebago, Calumet, Manitowoc, Fond du Lac, Sheboygan, Washington, and Ozaukee.

17. H. F. Gosnell, *Machine Politics*, pp. 107, 110 and *passim*.

18. *New York Times*, November 18, 1935, p. 1.

19. *Ibid.*, August 21, 1936, p. 1.

20. *Ibid.*, September 25, 1936, p. 1.

21. Wisconsin Regional Planning Commission, *op. cit.*, pp. 306-7.

22. *New York Times*, October 8, 1936, p. 1, and October 13, 1936, p. 23.

23. Cf. *ibid.*, October 15, 1936, p. 16. Turner Catledge: ''Except for the isolated case of the beef cattle raisers, the effect of the reciprocal trade agreements, including the one with Canada, doesn't amount to 'two whoops across the holler' in relation to the election Nov. 3.''

Ibid., October 22, 1936, p. 13. Arthur Krock: ''Nevertheless, the Republicans will make rural gains. They attribute this to Gov. Landon's tour, in which he stressed the treaty issue.''

Ibid., November 1, 1936, p. 32. "Dairy farmers generally are annoyed by the reciprocal trade treaty with Canada, and moreover, they did not participate as liberally as farmers of other states in AAA benefits."

24. *Ibid.*, September 26, 1936, p. 2.

25. Industrial Commission of Wisconsin, *Wisconsin Labor Market*, XVIII, No. 12 (December, 1938), p. 2.

26. *Wisconsin Public Welfare Review*, September, 1938, p. 6; also *ibid.*, June, 1938, p. 7.

27. At any rate, the correlation between the per cent of population unemployed in twenty-one non-agricultural counties of the state and per cent voting for Heil in those counties is —.82—a high negative relationship. Other economic indices bear out this result. Thus the correlation between the per cent on public assistance in the state's counties in September, 1938 and the per cent for Heil is —.68. The correlation between per cent for Heil with gross farm income in 1936 is .56, low compared to the two other measures but higher than any of the correlations involving economic indices arrived at in the presidential elections.

28. The data for per cent rural-farm and per cent native white are from the *Fifteenth Census of the United States.*

29. One way of getting at this problem is to correlate the per cent for a given candidate in an election with the per cent rural-farm, by counties. In the two presidential elections of the decade the coefficient of correlation of the Franklin Roosevelt vote with the per cent rural-farm was —.42 in 1932 and —.53 in 1936.

30. The per cent rural-farm population was related to various political variables as follows: with the percentage for La Follette, Sr., in the 1924 presidential race in a small positive fashion (r = +.38); with the vote for Blaine, progressive Republican senatorial candidate in 1926 in a similar positive fashion (r = +.40); with Phil La Follette's vote in 1930 in a negative fashion (r = —.31); in the 1932 primary in a positive manner (r = +.34); in 1934 and 1936 in a slightly positive fashion, and in the 1938 election not at all (r = .05).

31. With 2,500 to 10,000 and 10,000 to 25,000 population.

32. The coefficients of correlation between the per cent native white of native parentage and the percentage for Roosevelt were —.03 in 1932 and —.45 in 1936.

33. Gross farm income in 1936 correlated .51 with the per cent native white of native parentage.

34. In Iowa (see Chapter V, below) a similar rise is found in the correlations between the Roosevelt vote and the per cent native white of native parentage (—.39 for 1932 and —.62 for 1936). Here also the foreign vote was probably influenced by economic considerations. The most foreign areas of the state were those which had suffered the least from the drought between 1932 and 1936 while the predominately native white areas had suffered the most and reacted accordingly.

35. The correlation between the per cent for Heil, the Republican candidate, and this variable was +.52.

36. A. O. Barton, *La Follette's Winning of Wisconsin* (Madison, 1922), pp. 57-58. Various reasons for the adherence of Norwegians to La Follette are suggested here.

37. There is no basis for assuming that the same people voted for the national candidates of the party as for the state candidates, but we make the assumption that when there is a consistently high association of the two factors, there is strong indication of high party discipline.

38. REGULAR REPUBLICANS WITH REGULAR REPUBLICANS ('24-'38)

	r	Regression Equations	S
Hoover '28 and Kohler (Gov.) '28	.83	Y = 7.9 + .83X	5.8
Hoover '32 and Kohler (Gov.) '32	.86		
Chapple (Sen. '34) and Greene (Gov. '34)	.91	Y = 7.2 + .86X	3.1
Landon '36 and Wiley (Gov. '36)	.91		
Heil (Gov. '38) and Wiley (Sen. '38)	.86	Y = 9.8 + .91X	4.5

39. PROGRESSIVE REPUBLICANS WITH REGULAR REPUBLICANS ('24-'34)

	r	Regression Equations	S
Blaine (Gov. '24) and Coolidge ('24)	—.35	Y = 5.3 — .28X	8.0
R. La Follette, Jr. (Sen. '28) and Hoover ('28)	—.41	Y = 9.8 — .20X	4.6
P. La Follette (Gov. '39) and Hoover ('28)	.39		

40.

	r	Regression Equations	S
Blaine (Rep. Gov. '24) and La Follette, Sr. (Prog. Pres. '24)	.61	Y = 15.5 + .82X	4.8
R. La Follette, Jr. (Rep. Sen. '26) and La Follette, Sr. (Prog. Pres. '24)	.79		
R. La Follette, Jr. (Rep. Sen. '28) and Blaine (Sen. Rep. '26)	.56		
R. La Follette, Jr. (Prog. Sen. '34) and P. La Follette (Prog. Gov. '34)	.96	Y = 11.5 + .93X	2.4
Ekern (Prog. Sen. '38) and P. La Follette (Prog. Gov. '38)	.86	Y = —3.3 + .82X	4.8

41.

	r	Regression Equations	S
Roosevelt (Pres. '32) and Duffy (Sen. '32)	.91	Y = 13.1 + .89X	3.4
Duffy (Sen. '32) and Schmedeman (Gov. '32)	.89	Y = 5.6 + .96X	3.8

Callahan (Sen. '34) and Schmedeman
   (Gov. '32) .... .93 Y = −4.2 + .76X 2.7
Roosevelt (Pres. '36) and Lueck (Gov.
   '36) .... low by inspection of scatter
   Duffy (Sen. '38) and Bolens (Gov. '38.... .86 Y =   7.3 + 2.02X 4.59

42. Since the percentage of the votes of the Democratic and Progressive gubernatorial candidates combined is the complement of the percentage of the votes received by the Republican candidate, this would mean that the Progressive plus the Democratic vote would closely resemble the Roosevelt vote. We assume that the same people voted for Wiley as for Landon, and this assumption does not appear unduly unwarranted, especially since the vote for Wiley is only 4 per cent less than that for Landon in 1936. In Iowa in 1932, the number of votes for Roosevelt in any county was almost exactly equal to the votes for Al Smith in that county in 1928 plus the vote for the Progressive candidate for senator, Brookhart, in the 1932 primary. A regression equation for the 1936 election shows that the principal weight for the reelection of Roosevelt should be given to party tradition as measured by the 1932 Democratic presidential vote. Hence it can be said that in Iowa as well as Wisconsin, Roosevelt's reelection is due to a Democratic-Progressive alliance. See H. F. Gosnell and Norman Pearson, ''The Study of Voting Behavior by Correlation Techniques,'' *American Sociological Review*, .IV, No. 6 (December, 1939), pp. 809-15.

43. *New York Times*, August 19, 1936, pp. 14-15.

44. r = .86 (a = 9.8, b = .91, S = 4.54, σ = 8.94). The discipline between the two Progressive candidates, Phil La Follette and Ekern, was only slightly lower, while the Democratic party exhibited a very weak organization. The Democratic candidate for governor, Bolens, received only 9 per cent of the total vote, while his running mate, Duffy, got 25 per cent of the senatorial vote.

45. The coefficient of correlation between Henry's total vote in the primary (both Republican and Democratic) as a percentage of the total primary vote and the percentage vote for Heil in the general election was +.70.

46. Let X_e = per cent for Henry (Democratic and Republican) of total
             primary vote
    X_f = per cent native white of native parentage
    X_g = per cent of population on relief
    X_h = average gross farm increase 1936
    Then r_{ef} = .42; r_{eg} = −.27; r_{eh} = .33

47. Correlations:

	Rep.	Dem.	Prog.
Gov. 1934-1936	.84	.84	.81
Gov. 1936-1938	.56	.75	.84
Sen. 1934-1938	.58	.78	.61
Dem. Pres. 1936 and Rep. Gov. 1934	−.77		
Dem. Pres. 1936 and Rep. Gov. 1936	−.91		
Dem. Pres. 1936 and Rep. Gov. 1938	−.46		

48. The fifteen traditionally Democratic counties, in approximate order of strength of party tradition, are Ozaukee, Milwaukee, Portage, Langlade, Brown, Calumet, Dodge, Manitowoc, Washington, Jefferson, Kewaunee, Fond du Lac, Green Lake, Forest, and Crawford.

49. Buffalo, Burnett, Taylor, Trempealeau, Ashland, Monroe, Iron, Bayfield, Adams, Jackson, Barron, Shawano, Polk, Washburn, Vernon.

50. Walworth, Rock, Florence, Richland, Dunn, Pierce, St. Croix, Eau Claire, Rusk, Waupaca, Waushara, Grant, Iowa, Chippewa, and Pepin.

CHAPTER V

1. Table VII (See Appendix II) shows the closeness of the vote. In 1912 Woodrow Wilson won the electoral votes of Iowa although he polled only a minority of the popular votes. See also: J. A. Neprash, *Brookhart Campaigns in Iowa* (New York, 1932).

2. See Chapter II, note 18. above.

3. H. Bowen, *Iowa Income* (Ames, 1935), 36.

4. Iowa State Planning Board, *A Preliminary Report of Progress* (Detroit, 1934), p. 246.

5. T. W. Schultz, ''Agricultural Economic Conditions in Iowa,'' *Yearbook of Agriculture*, 1935.

6. See Table IX, Appendix II.

7. Thus, though in 1932 a bumper crop was produced, the farmer could not even make production expenses because of the low prices.

8. *Iowa Yearbook of Agriculture*, 1939, p. 15.

9. Iowa State Planning Board, *The Second Report* (1935), pp. 27-28.

10. Schultz, *op. cit.*, p. 268.

11. The trend is strongly toward an agricultural ''proletariat.'' According to the U. S. Census for 1930, there were 89,165 farm laborers in Iowa, not including unpaid family workers. These comprised 26.9 per cent of all employed in agriculture and 51.5 per cent in the number engaged in manufacturing (173,149).

12. Iowa State Department of Agriculture, *Iowa Yearbook of Agriculture*, 1932 (Des Moines, 1933), p. 6.

13. See Table VII, Appendix II.

14. Henry Wallace, *America Must Choose* (New York, 1933).

15. *Iowa Yearbook of Agriculture*, 1939, p. 266.

16. These terms refer to the five economic sections of the state as defined by the United States Department of Agriculture.

17. The dairy area and the eastern central meat area show, for the most part, less pronounced losses.

18. Iowa State Planning Board, *Sescond Report*, pp. 84-85, 276.

19. Schultz, *op. cit.*, p. 269.

20. Iowa State Planning Board, *Preliminary Report*, p. 36.

21. *Ibid.*, pp. 248-262.

22. Schultz, *op. cit.*, pp. 278-85.

23. *Ibid.*, p. 56.

24. *Iowa Yearbook of Agriculture*, 1934, p. 7.

25. *Ibid.*, p. 245.

26. Highest September 15 average since 1929 was reached on September 15, 1936, when the Iowa farm price index was 136 per cent of the pre-war average.

27. *New York Times*, November 10, 1940, IV, p. 4.

28. The rural farm population in 1930, however, comprised only about 39 per cent of the total population. See the United States Census, 1930, Volume III.

29. Where political parties are differentiated on the basis of principles, a much stronger presumption as to the relationship is established. In Iowa, as in most states, the straddling Democratic and Republican parties dominate the scene.

30. Neprash (*op. cit.*, 75) considered the use of the Iowa counties as units in correlation highly questionable. He held that they were largely responsible for his low coefficients.

31. Neprash, *op. cit.*, 73.

32. Neprash never distinguished his economic indexes in time, but he did include such indexes as ''value of crops per farm,'' ''value of all domestic animals per farm,'' and ''bank deposits per capita'' which can be considered indexes of income in the immediate year. See *op. cit.*, p. 73. Though banking accounts were carried by about 80 per cent of the rural population in 1929, samplings of the Planning Board showed only 42 per cent in 1934 (see the *Second Report* of the Iowa State Planning Board, p. 198). For the 1930's this index would not be representative enough.

33. Thus, an average shift of 22.6 per cent occurred from Smith in 1928 to Roosevelt in 1932. The mixed shifts from 1932 to 1936 were large enough to change the political density maps considerably.

34. The *Iowa Yearbook of Agriculture*, 1936, gives the distribution of corn and livestock production per county for each year. Marketing figures would, of course, have been better.

35. Corn is really the more basic of the two, for the number of hogs raised in most counties depends upon the amount of corn raised. Because of the fact that the southern and dairy counties didn't follow this function, but rather tended to produce more hogs than was expected from the corn production, the hog index was dropped. This may have been due to the fact that the cash grain area shipped its corn at the high price rather than feed it to livestock.

36. It is assumed that the 1935 production was close to ''normal''; however, it would undoubtedly be better to take a long-time average because of the AAA and other short-run fluctuations.

37. The coefficient of correlation was found to be plus .49. This is not very high, but it shows that Roosevelt lost votes where the corn losses were greatest.

A scatter diagram was constructed between the corn index and the Roosevelt 1936 vote and revealed no relation at all; hence partials holding the total density vote constant would not appreciably reduce the coefficient obtained from the net shifts in the vote and corn production.

On the coefficient of correlation: regression equation, standard error, and standard deviation:

X_h = net shift in Roosevelt vote, 1932-1936

X_c = net shift in corn production, 1935-1936

X_h = plus .5 + .12 X_c S_{hc} = 3.80 σ_h = 4.97

r_{hc} = .49

38. It is for this reason that not only will a long-run economic index give a zero or very low positive or negative coefficient of correlation, but, in addition, the income index for 1936 will give only a very low relation with the full density distribution of Roosevelt's 1936 vote (r = .10).

39. The equation which expresses the Roosevelt vote as a function of the other two variables gives an almost perfect fit to the data. (r = —.78 between Coolidge and Smith vote). That Roosevelt drew the same discontented element in 1932 which had been stirred up after 1929 is shown by r = —.81 for Coolidge and Roosevelt.

40. Let X_o = the actual number of votes received by Roosevelt in 1932

X_p = the actual number of votes received by Al Smith in 1928

X_q = the actual number of votes received by Brookhart in the Republican primary of 1932

Then: X_o = 3.17 + 1.16 X_p + .88X_q, σ = 46.51

$S_{o \cdot pq}$ = 8.42

$R_{o \cdot pq}$ = .98

(The relationship is somewhat accentuated by a few extreme cases in the distribution of actual votes.)

41. The following eleven elections were included in calculating the county averages: presidential elections for 1924, 1928, 1932, and 1936, United States senatorial elections for 1926, 1932, and 1936, and gubernatorial elections for 1930, 1932, 1934, and 1936.

42. Table VII of this book gives the mean county percentages for Roosevelt's vote in 1936 and 1940. The difference between them is 9.0 per cent.

43. The vote on the AAA in October 1935, when plotted on a scatter diagram with the Roosevelt 1936 vote, showed a slight positive relation and the southern counties were among those weakest in support of the AAA.

44. W. F. Ogburn and N. S. Talbot, ''A Measurement of the Factors in the Presidential Election of 1928,'' *Social Forces*, VIII, No. 2 (1929).

45. The coefficient between this vote and the Roosevelt vote was .55.

46. Notice that these counties cut across the economic boundary between the well-to-do southern part of the western meat area and the western part of the poor southern pasture area.

47. Neprash, *op. cit.*

48. $r_{ot} = .81$ for President (X_o) with senator (X_t)
$r_{og} = .66$ for President with governor (X_g)
$X_o = 20.1 + .72X_t$ $\qquad$ $S_{ot} = 3.75$ $\quad$ $\sigma_o = 6.37$
$X_o = 34.7 + .49 X_g$ $\qquad$ $S_{og} = 4.81$

It can be seen from these measures that most of the splitting occurred with respect to the vote for governor.

49. $r_{ij} = .96$ President (X_i) with Senator (X_j)
$r_{ik} = .91$ President with Governor (X_k)
$X_i = -.2 + 1.08 X_j$ $\quad$ $S_i.j = 1.71$
$X_i = 5.2 + 1.01 X_k$ $\quad$ $S_i.k = 2.53$ $\qquad$ $\sigma_j = 6.11$

These measures reveal clearly a much higher interrelationship in 1936 than in 1932. The 1938 congressional election indicated a considerable break in party discipline.

50. In the 1938 congressional election Guy M. Gillette (Democrat) won the senatorial election against Dickinson (Republican) by a very slight margin and George A. Wilson (Republican) won the governorship.

51. The Roosevelt 1940 losses in the farm states contiguous to Iowa (net shifts 1936-1940) were much greater than in Iowa—Nebraska, 15 per cent; South Dakota, 13 per cent; Minnesota, 15 per cent; and Wisconsin, 17 per cent. Table VIII shows that the Roosevelt loss in Iowa was 8 per cent. Wallace's presence on the Democratic ticket may have helped the Roosevelt ticket to the extent of 5 per cent.

52. Let X_s = Roosevelt's percentage of the major party vote in 1940
X_t = percentage of major party vote for governor in 1904 received by Democratic candidate, Valentine
X_i = Roosevelt's percentage of the total vote in 1936
then the following relationships are obtained:
$r_{si} = .64$ $\qquad$ $X_s = 9.01 + .68X_i$
$r_{st} = .93$ $\qquad$ $X_s = -.91 + 1.04 X_t$

53. This may be done by the standard technique of net regression. Thus the 1936 Roosevelt percentage in each county may be said to be made up of a constant, 37, plus three-fourths of his 1932 percentage, less 7 per cent of the wet percentage, less 12 per cent of the rural-farm percentage, plus 7 per cent of the corn loss, less 19 per cent of the percentage of native white of native parentage.

Let X_i = Roosevelt's percentage of the total vote in 1936
X_n = the percentage in favor of repeal in 1935
X_m = the rural farm percentage in 1930

X_v = corn loss, 1935-36

X_w = the percentage native white of native parentage

then the following function results:

$X_1 = 37.0690 + .7307 X_e - .0661 X_n - .1163 X_m + .0680 X_v - .1921 X_w$

$S_1 . _{enmvw} = 3.3824$ $R_1 . _{enmvw} = .83$

For the 99 Iowa counties, this formula according to the method of least squares, will give the closest approximation to the 1936 vote of any possible formula using these variables. The meaning of this equation is reasonably clear but there may be some doubt as to the interpretation of the constant. Since there are no cases near the zero end of any of the variable scales, the reliability of the absolute value of the constant, a, cannot be very great. The equation holds only for the limited range of data used in this study. A common sense interpretation of the rather high constant would be that the 1936 Roosevelt percentage did not fall below 37 in any county of the state (actual minimum vote was 41 per cent in Page County).

54. What is left of the equation indicates the relationship of the shifts in the Roosevelt percentage from 1932 to 1936 to the variables studied.

55. See H. F. Gosnell, *Machine Politics*.

56. The coefficient ($r_{1e} = .68$) may be interpreted as meaning that the two votes in the 99 counties have 47 per cent of their variations ($r^2_{1e} = .47$) in common. ($r_{1n} = .55$, $r_{en} = .46$)

57. $r_{1m} = -.02$, $r_{em} = .30$

58. $r_{1v} = .10$, $r_{ev} = -.28$

59. $r_{1w} = -.62$, $r_{ew} = -.39$

60. The fourth-order coefficients of partial correlation give an idea of the relationship of each of the variables to the 1936 Roosevelt percentage when all other variables are held constant.

61. $r_{1e.wvnm} = .67$, $r_{1w.evnm} = -.55$, $r_{1v.ewnm} = .30$, $r_{1n.ewvm} = -.19$, $r_{1m.ewvn} = -.18$.

62. Use of technique of net regression. In this equation the 1936 Roosevelt percentage (X_1) is the dependent variable and the other variables are the independent ones. The relatively high value for the parameter involving the 1932 Roosevelt percentage ($b_{1e.wvnm} = .73$) agrees with the coefficient of partial correlation. The remaining parameters describe the characteristics of the voters who did change.

63. The equation justifies this hypothesis since a close examination of its parameters shows that they resemble quite closely the parameters for the preceding equation.

X_1 = shift from 1932 to 1936 as expressed by the difference between the percentages

$X_1 = 27.4315 - .1330 X_n - .1660 X_m + .1003 X_v - .1790 X_w$

$S_{1.nmvw} = 4.12$ $R_{1.nmvw} = .56$

CHAPTER VI

1. F. W. Bisbee, "Governor Olson's Victory," *New Republic*, XCVII, (February 22, 1939), p. 76; H. Chandler, "Viewpoint of Southern California," *Review of Reviews*, XCIII, March, 1936), 40; Walter Davenport, "California, Here We Come," *Collier's* XCVI (August 10, 1935), 10, and "Sinclair Gets the Glory Vote," *Collier's*, XCIV (October 27, 1934), 12; T. Rodriguez and W. G. Fennell, "Agrarian Revolt in California," *Nation*, CXXXVII (September 6, 1933), 272; S. Simpich, "Northern California at Work," *National Geographic* LXIX (March, 1936), pp. 309-89, and "Southern California at Work," *National Geographic*, LXVI (November, 1934), pp. 529-600; Lillian Symes, "California There She Stands," *Harpers*, CLXX (February, 1935), p. 360.

2. The coefficient of correlation between the percentage for Coolidge in 1924 and the percentage for Roosevelt in 1932 was —.82.

3. The coefficient of correlation between the per cent for Coolidge and per cent rural-farm was —.22. The coefficient of correlation between per cent for Coolidge and per cent pro-repeal was —.47.

4. For a discussion of farm labor conditions in California, see Carey Mc-Williams, *Factories in the Fields* (Boston, 1939).

5. *New York Times*, December 23, 1928, Section III, p. 2.

6. California State Emergency Relief Administration, *Monthly Bulletin on Relief Activities and Statistics*, Vol I, Number 6. (San Francisco, December, 1934), pp. 6-7.

7. Federal Writers' Project of California (W.P.A.), *California, A Guide to the Golden State* (New York, 1939), p. 106.

8. The coefficient of correlation between the votes of the two was +.73.

9. *New York Times*, September 29, 1932, p. 12.

10. Correlation was +.89.

11. Wisconsin is an outstanding example.

12. In most cases the correlations are too low to have any significance, and in some cases they are actually negative.

13. Deering's *General Laws of the State of California*.

14. Deering's *Political Code of the State of California*, S1096a.

15. Dean McHenry, "Legislative Personnel in California," *Annals of the American Academy of Political and Social Science* (January, 1938).

CHAPTER VII

1. An excellent discussion of metropolitan under-representation and disfranchisement in Illinois may be found in Albert Lepawsky, *Home Rule For Metropolitan Chicago* (Chicago, 1935), pp. 148-55. See also Illinois Legislative Council, *Reapportionment in Illinois* (Springfield).

2. See map, "Population Trends by Counties 1890 to 1930," *Report of the Illinois State Planning Commission* (Springfield, 1934 and 1935), p. 31.

3. Lepawsky, *op. cit.*, p. xv.

4. R. L. Mott, "Reapportionment in Illinois," *American Political Science Review*, XXI (August, 1927), p. 598.

5. See Table XII, Appendix, for relevant figures.

6. Chapter II, note 14.

7. See Table XII, above.

8. For a fuller discussion of this point see H. F. Gosnell, *Machine Politics*. See also M. S. Mayer, "Chicago Doesn't Care," *Nation*, vol. 146 (February, 1938), pp. 561-71, and T. Leitzell, "Chicago, City of Corruption," *American Mercury*, XL (February, 1940), pp. 143-51.

9. H. F. Gosnell, *Machine Politics*, pp. 12-26.

10. The Kelly-Nash machine lost the nomination for Cook county judge in 1938.

11. See Table XII, above.

12. In the 1924 Republican senatorial primary, the vote between Charles S. Deneen and Medill McCormick was very close. Deneen won because he had a 10,000 plurality in Cook County. In the 1926 Democratic senatorial primary, George Brennan got an overwhelming majority in Cook County and only a plurality downstate. Running for the same office in 1928, Anton J. Cermak got an overwhelming vote in Cook County but lost downstate. In the 1932 Democratic gubernatorial primary, Horner won Cook County by a large margin, but lost downstate to Michael Igoe. In the 1936 and 1938 Democratic primaries the winning majorities were found downstate.

13. The materials for this and the following two paragraphs were adapted from *Machine Politics, op. cit.*, pp. 21-24.

14. *Chicago Evening American*, March 28, 1936.

15. For a discussion of the units used see *Machine Politics, op. cit.*, pp. 92-106, 195-201.

16. The interrelationships between the variables are expressed in the form of coefficients of correlation as in the preceding chapters. The correlation matrix for 101 downstate Illinois counties is given in Table XIII.

17. The agricultural regions in Illinois have been outlined in the *Report of the Illinois State Planning Commission*, 1934, p. 48.

18. "The Ever-Normal County," *Fortune*, XXI (June, 1940), p. 86.

19. It is hard to isolate the farm vote in this region. Some of the farmers are part-time coal miners.

20. Illinois State Planning Commission, *op. cit.*, p. 67.

21. Figures 14 and 15 show a strong Republican bias among the voters in the counties adjoining Chicago (Cook county).

22. The coefficient of correlation between Al Smith votes and the per cent rural-farm was almost zero (.03). An examination of the maps or scatter diagrams shows that of the counties with cities over 50,000, four (Peoria, Winnebago, Sangamon, and Macon) were strongly Republican in 1928 and one (St. Clair) was Democratic.

23. The coal counties are Franklin, Macoupin, Perry, Saline, and Williamson.

24. The following have been classified as the oil counties: Clinton, Crawford, Effingham, Fayette, Jasper, Jefferson, Lawrence, Marion, Richland, and Wabash. Chicago *Tribune*, July 17, 1940.

25. The coefficients in Table XIII show that the relationship between the votes and the percentage on relief was below .40 until the election of 1938, when the coefficient was .52.

26. The relationship between the per cent Democratic and the per cent voting wet downstate was very low during the thirties, whereas in Chicago the relationship was still high (coefficient over .60).

27. The proportion of native white of native parentage is so high in most of the downstate counties that it is very difficult to study the influence of foreign extraction by correlation methods.

28. The political complexion of the southern part of the state has been influenced by migration from the Solid Democratic South.

29. The coefficient of correlation for per cent Democratic in 1936 presidential election and per cent Catholic in 1926 was .08 in Illinois downstate counties, .36 in Pennsylvania counties and for Chicago .78 (per cent of foreign stock from Catholic countries).

30. These in general are the same counties which have a high proportion of native whites of native parentage. ($r_{ad} = -.55$).

31. Table XII contains all the relevant figures. For a discussion of these trends in Chicago alone see *Machine Politics, op. cit.*, p. 94.

32. The coefficients of correlation may be found in Table XIII. The comparable coefficients for the 144 Chicago districts are found in *Machine Politics*, 109, 124.

33. For instance, the relationship between the Smith and 1936 Roosevelt votes in Chicago was quite close (r = .88) but in downstate counties the relationship was not so close (r = .66). A comparison of the Illinois maps shows the relationship between the Smith and 1936 Roosevelt votes in Illinois was about the same as in Wisconsin (see note 42, Chapter IV, r = .68). However, the relationship between the 1932 and 1936 Roosevelt votes in downstate Illinois was as close as in Pennsylvania (r = .78).

34. For downstate counties the coefficient of correlation between the Democratic percentages for president and governor in 1932 was .82, for Chicago area, .44.

35. In 1936 the coefficient of correlation between the Democratic percentages for president and governor in the Illinois downstate counties was .96. The coefficient for the Pennsylvania counties between the Democratic candidates for president and for state treasurer in 1936 was .99.

36. The zero order coefficients are arranged in the order of their magnitude regardless of signs and then squared. This process gives the coefficient of determination which indicates the proportion of the variations which the dependent and independent variables have in common. See Appendix I, above for discussion. Because of insufficient funds, an equation of net regression was not calculated for Illinois.

37. Table XIII gives the relevant figures from which coefficients of partial correlation might be calculated.

CHAPTER VIII

1. A sample group in Louisiana was asked by Gallup investigators in December 1939, ''Do you think elections in Louisiana in recent years have been honestly conducted?'' Twenty-five per cent answered ''Yes,'' sixty per cent answered ''No,'' and fifteen per cent had no opinion. George Gallup and Saul Forbes Rae, *The Pulse of Democracy* (New York, 1940), p. 156. For a factual basis for the prevalent opinion, see U. S. Senate, *The Hearings of the Special Committee on Investigation of Campaign Expenditures*, 72nd Congress, 2nd session (1932), and *Report* No. 191, 73rd Congress, 2nd session.

2. Paul Lewinson, *Race, Class and Party* (London, 1932), p. 81.

3. *Ibid.*

4. *Report of Secretary of State of Louisiana*, 1937-1938, table affixed.

5. Lewinson, *op. cit.*, p. 230.

6. *United States Census of Religious Bodies*, 1926, p. 1256.

7. See, among others: Howard W. Odum, *Southern Regions of the United States* (Chapel Hill: University of North Carolina, 1936); Mary Mims and G. W. Moritz, *The Awakening Community* (New York, 1932); Harnett T. Kane, *Louisiana Hayride* (New York, 1941); Gallup and Rae, *op. cit.*, chap. 13, and W. J. Cash, *The Mind of the South* (New York, 1941).

8. In 43 out of 64 parishes, one-half or more of all farmers were tenants in 1930. Odum, *op. cit.*, p. 254.

9. One is reminded here of the medieval poem by Henricus of Erfurt:

''The pestilence like fury broke,
And took its thousands from our folk;
The earth against us fiercely turned—
And many Jews were therefore burned.''

The Negro substitutes for the medieval Jew in Louisiana.

10. Odum, *op. cit.*, p. 146. The rates for rape and aggravated assault were medium with reference to the other states, those for auto theft, burglary, larceny, and robbery were lower than the national average. The latter rates may be the result of poverty. Figures are for cities and towns, not rural areas—a significant omission which destroys much of the efficacy of the reports. One must add, too, that the criminal statistics of the Bureau of Census are not as reliable as most other materials they present. The relationship between voting behavior and antisocial behavior is an untouched field. Hints have been given us, however. See e.g., Wayne Dennis, ''Differential Social Characteristics of Convicted Automobile Drivers,'' *Ohio State University Studies*, 1930, pp. 114-131, and ''Traits Associated with Registration and Voting,'' *Journal of Abnormal and Social Psychiatry*, XXVII (October-December, 1932), p. 270.

11. Odum, *op. cit.*, p. 102.

12. Carleton Beals, *The Story of Huey P. Long* (New York, 1935), chap. XXIV.

13. ''The South [of Louisiana] is tolerant, easy-going, Catholic. The North is tight-lipped, grim-eyed, Puritan, Protestant. Between the 'hard-shelled Baptist country' and the 'soft-shelled crab land' are barriers of economics, of race, of creed. In each there is want among the many, but with this difference—that it is differently accepted. In the North it has brought cankering hatred; it has meant lynchings of Negroes, membership in organizations of dissent, anti-Papism, anti-liquor, anti many things. In the South it has meant volatile debate, perhaps; but that has ended in quiet if regretful assumption of the burden with a shrug and an 'Eh bien.' '' Kane, *op. cit.*, p. 31.

14. *Representative Government* (1861), Everyman Edition, p. 218.

15. See Lewinson, *op. cit.;* W. F. Fleming, *Documentary History of Reconstruction*, 2 vols. (Cleveland, 1906); J. K. Ficklen, *History of Reconstruction in Louisiana* (Baltimore, 1910); Ella Lonn, *Reconstruction in Louisiana after 1868* (New York, 1918); Henry Clay Warmoth, *War, Politics and Reconstruction; Stormy Days in Louisiana* (New York, 1930); W. M. Coskey, *Secession and Restoration of Louisiana* (University, La.), 1938).

16. Odum, *op. cit.*, p. 135.

17. With euphemism prompted by political necessity, one writer on Louisiana government who taught at Louisiana State University wrote: ''Most powerful of all the forces at work is the Governor, the influence of the present encumbent has been exceedingly weighty and he has interested himself in practically every legislative matter, some of which have been relatively minor in character . . . . he is constantly consulted by representatives and senators who seek his advice.'' Melvin Adams, *A Study in the State Government of Louisiana* (Baton Rouge, 1931), pp. 121-122.

The *New Orleans Times-Picayune* (September 13, 1935), in discussing the laws enacted at Long's last special session, remarked ''All were passed at hurricane speed, without pretense of consideration and debate, with the law-giving majorities in general as ignorant of their content, purpose, and effect as their constituents back home.''

18. The principles and platform of the ''Share-the-Wealth'' movement are found in a pamphlet entitled *Share Our Wealth:* (1) ''To limit poverty by providing that every deserving family shall share in the wealth of America for not less than one-third of the average wealth, thereby to possess not less than $5,000 free of debt.'' (2) ''To limit fortunes to such few million dollars as will allow the balance of the American people to share in the wealth and profits of the land.'' (3) ''Old-age pensions of $30 per month to persons over sixty years of age who do not earn as much as $1,000 per year or who possess less than $10,000 in cash or property, thereby to remove from the field of labor in times of unemployment those who have contributed their share to the public service.'' (4) ''To limit the hours of work to such an extent as to prevent over-production and to give the workers of America some share in the recreations, conveniences, and luxuries of life.'' (5) ''To balance agricultural production with what can be sold and consumed according to the laws of God, which have never failed.'' (6) ''To care for the veterans of our wars.'' (7) ''Taxation to run the government to be supported, first by reducing big fortunes from the top, thereby to improve the country and provide employment in public works whenever agricultural surplus is such as to render unnecessary, in whole or in part, any particular crop.''

19. Raymond Gram Swing, *Forerunners of American Fascism* (New York, 1935), pp. 72-3.

20. Carleton Beals, *op. cit.,* pp. 59-60.

21. Cash, *op. cit.,* p. 285.

22. Huey Long was born in the small town of Winnfield in Winn Parish, August 30, 1893. The parish, located in the north central part of the state, is not a typical section of the state; it more closely resembles the red-clay hill sections of Alabama, Georgia, or Mississippi. It is a denuded, infertile, dilapidated landscape, furnishing a bare living for poor white cotton farmers and emancipated Negroes. Huey Long's family was like any average ''red-neck'' product of the deflated South of post-reconstruction days. Huey's father, a farmer, was distinguished from the majority of his neighbors in that he eked out a menial living from his cotton crop without the aid of Negroes or the handicap of a landlord.

Huey Long's early life was spent at hard work and was not marked by any unusual qualities or characteristics. He did not finish secondary school, and indeed, often remarked that his only education came from reading the Bible, the classics, and Roman law. He started to work at the age of eighteen, and after trying his hand at salesmanship for some time, finally got together enough money to take an intensive law course at Tulane University in New Orleans for one year. The responsibilities of marriage had meanwhile been added to those of making a living. After completing his law course, he persuaded the State Bar Commission to give him a special examination, which he passed in 1914. Returning to his home town, he went into partnership with his brother. It was an unsuccessful combination and after three years Huey began building up a sizeable practice and a growing reputation for himself. In 1918 he was elected to the Public Service Commission of Louisiana. He made the most of his opportunity and succeeded in attracting more publicity, all the time keeping his ear to the ground for bigger things.

Doubtless the key to Long's success lies as much in his psychological traits as in the existing milieu. His chief traits were an overwhelming hunger for power, vindictiveness, anti-authoritarianism and feeling for the underdog, and strategic daring combined with physical cowardice. These may be mentioned, although a thorough analysis of his character would modify and refine them. A worthwhile procedure would be to apply to his life the framework of traits devised by the author and Mr. Sebastian De Grazia for the analysis of successful and unsuccessful presidential candidates. This would undoubtedly explain in greater detail and clarity the ramifications of Long's personality, and, by tracing the origins of his traits, point out the organic relationship between the northern Louisiana environment and the Long type of politician.

23. The index chosen to measure the economic status of a parish was the productivity of land per capita farm operator.

24. Long's New Orleans vote increased, among other reasons, by virtue of his alliance with John Sullivan, attorney with racing and related connections, and Robert Ewing, publisher, both of whom had broken with The Old Ring.

25. Carroll Hill Wooddy, *The Case of Frank L. Smith* (Chicago, 1931), Appendix V.

26. Beals, *op. cit.*, p. 83.

27. The scatter-diagrams show that different Long candidates received their strength from different parts of the state.

28. We can quote in this regard the findings of Wooddy (*op. cit.*, p. 380) and qualify it with relation to Huey Long's votes with an ''only more so'' and with relation to the Long machine from 1936-1940 with an ''only less so.'' ''It is assumed often that 'machines' constructed by dominant political leaders who remain in power for a series of years are more or less permanent, i.e., that the same voters, or the same groups of counties, support them in successive elections. Elsewhere in the text it has been suggested that the converse is true; that machines are more or less evanescent, the support gained by candidates in particular elections depending upon combinations made for the purpose of that election. . . . [The writer proceeds to give evidence for the latter thesis.] This evidence taken in conjunction with the evidence set forth in chaps. iii and vi, indicates conclusively that Smith did not have a large block of downstate counties upon which he could consistently count for support during his recent career.''

29. Gallup and Rae, *op. cit.*, pp. 156-57.

30. See Table XIV, Appendix II, for a comparison of New Orleans with the rest of the state in the various electiones.

The pro-Long candidates were Huey P. Long, Governor, 1924; Hewitt Bouanchaud in the run-off for Governor, 1924; Joseph Ransdell for Senator, 1924; Edwin Broussard for Senator, 1926; Huey P. Long for Governor, 1928; Huey P. Long for Senator, 1930; Oscar K. Allen for Governor, 1932; John H. Overton for Senator, 1932; Richard W. Leche for Governor, 1936; Allen J. Ellender for Senator, 1936; Oscar K. Allen for Senator (unexpired term), 1936; Earl K. Long for Governor in the regular primary and run-off, 1940.

31. The best complete account of the breakdown of the Long machine is to be found in Kane, *op. cit.*

32. The American Institute of Public Opinion polled Louisiana citizens in December 1939. The interviewers asked, ''Taking everything into consideration, do you think that Huey P. Long was a bad or a good influence in Louisiana?'' The results were: Good Influence, 55 per cent; Bad Influence, 22 per cent; both Good and Bad, 14 per cent; no opinion, 9 per cent. Gallup and Rae, *op. cit.*, pp. 157-58.

33. On June 30, 1941, Louisiana's Supreme Court annulled the legislative act and constitutional amendment whereunder the state government was reorganized for economy and efficiency. The majority decision turned on technical defects both in the reorganization statute and in the act submitting the authorizing amendment to the constitution which had been duly ratified by Louisiana's voters. (Full decision in the *New Orleans Times-Picayune*, July 1, 1941.) Noe left the ranks of the Jones reformers, thereby weakening them considerably.

CHAPTER IX

1. Walter Lippmann, *An Inquiry Into the Principles of a Good Society* (Boston, 1937), p. 108.

2. Lawrence Dennis, *The Dynamics of War and Revolution* (Weekly Foreign Letter, 1940), p. xii.

3. Daniel Katz, ''The Public Opinion Poll and the 1940 Election,'' *The Public Opinion Quarterly*, V (March, 1941), 52-78.

4. Edward H. Litchfield, *Voting Behavior in a Metropolitan Area* (University of Michigan, Ann Arbor, Michigan, 1941), p. 7.

5. *Machine Politics: Chicago Model* (Chicago, 1937).

6. See Silas Bent, ''Will the Democrats Follow the Whigs?'' *Scribner's Magazine*, Vol. 86 (November, 1929), p. 473.

7. W. F. Ogburn and N. S. Talbot, ''A Measurement of the Factors in the Presidential Election of 1928,'' *Social Forces*, VIII (December, 1929).

8. Pennsylvania furnishes a good example of this change. Until the New

Deal it was assumed that the men who paid for the campaigns, the coal, steel, oil, and railroad interests, could run the government. (See Walter Davenport, *Power and Glory: The Life of Boies Penrose* (New York, 1931). But in 1938, of the fifteen counties returning the highest percentage vote for Earle, all but one (Greene, a traditionally Democratic county) were industrial and mining counties.

9.   J. T. Salter, "Letters from Men in Action II," *National Municipal Review*, XXX (August, 1941), 471.

10.   *Forty Years on Main Street* (New York, 1937), p. 77.

11.   "We the People," *Fortune Magazine*, XXI, No. 4 (April, 1940), 64.

12.   (New York, 1941), pp. 259-60.

13.   For an analysis of New Jersey politics consult D. D. McKean, *The Boss: The Hague Machine in Action* (Boston:

14.   The Communist vote in that year was 103,152 for the whole of the United States, or .0026 per cent of the total.

15.   Only a few works describing subversive activities in the United States can be cited here: D. S. Strong, *Organized Anti-Semitism in America; The Rise of Group Prejudice During the Decade 1930-1940;* (Washington, D. C.: American Council on Public Affairs, 1941); Bulletins of Institute of Propaganda Analysis; *Fortune Magazine* (article on the foreign language press, 1940, vol. 22, pp. 90-93); Harold Lavine, *War Propaganda in the United States* (Institute for Propaganda Analysis; New Haven, 1940); Richard Rollins, *I Find Treason* (New York, 1941); Gaetano Salvemini, *Italian Fascist Activities in the United States* (American Council on Public Affairs, 1940).

16.   Hearings, Subcommittee of the Committee on Education and Labor, U. S. Senate, 74th Congress, 2nd Session (U. S. Government Printing Office, 1936).

INDEX

187